UNITED STATES
HISTORY ATLAS

HAMMOND INCORPORATED, MAPLEWOOD, NEW JERSEY

Contents

Gazetteer of States, Territories and Possessions ⸺ U-3
Native Americans ⸺ U-4
Voyages of Discovery to America ⸺ U-5
Voyages of Discovery to Asia and Africa ⸺ U-5
Early Maps of the New World ⸺ U-6
Exploration of the United States ⸺ U-6
European Settlements on the North American Coast 1500–1600 ⸺ U-7
European Powers in the New World ⸺ U-7
Early Colonial Grants ⸺ U-8–9
French and Indian Wars 1689–1763 ⸺ U-10–11
France and Spain in Interior North America before 1763 ⸺ U-11
Colonial America 1770 ⸺ U-12–13
Colonial California 1769–1823 ⸺ U-13
The American Revolution 1775–1781 ⸺ U-14–15
Settlement of the United States 1770–1890 ⸺ U-16
Expansion of the United States 1783–1898 ⸺ U-16
Conflicting Claims to the West after the Treaty of 1783 ⸺ U-17
The War of 1812 ⸺ U-18–19
Naval Battles 1777–1815 ⸺ U-19
Operations Against the Barbary States 1803–1815 ⸺ U-19
Early Transportation 1783–1860 ⸺ U-20
The Texas Revolution 1835–1836 ⸺ U-21
The Mexican War 1846–1848 ⸺ U-21
Free and Slave Areas 1821–1861 ⸺ U-22–23
The Civil War 1861–1865 ⸺ U-24–25
Slaves 1860; Cotton Production 1860 ⸺ U-25
The Virginia Campaigns of the Civil War 1861–1865 ⸺ U-26–27
The Battle of Gettysburg ⸺ U-27
Reconstruction Period 1865–1877 ⸺ U-28
Black Participation in Constitutional Conventions 1867–1868 ⸺ U-28
Rich States and Poor States 1860 vs. 1880 ⸺ U-29
The West 1860–1912 ⸺ U-30–31
Indian Reservations and Army Posts in the West ⸺ U-31
The Spanish-American War 1898 ⸺ U-32
The United States in Middle America ⸺ U-32–33
The United States in Latin America ⸺ U-33
Growth of Industry and Cities ⸺ U-34–35

Tariff Rates on Dutiable Imports ⸺ U-36
Foreign Trade ⸺ U-36
Exports; Imports ⸺ U-37
Sources of Immigration ⸺ U-38
Immigration Patterns of Major Foreign Groups 1821–1921 ⸺ U-38
Total Immigration from all Countries ⸺ U-38
Distribution of Foreign Born in United States 1910 ⸺ U-39
World War I in Europe ⸺ U-40
The Western Front ⸺ U-40
The Western Front 1918, Reduction of the Salients and Final Offensive ⸺ U-41
Europe in the 1920's ⸺ U-41
The Great Depression ⸺ U-42–43
Conservation of Natural Resources ⸺ U-44–45
German Expansion 1935–1939 ⸺ U-46
World War II 1939–1940 ⸺ U-46
World War II, European Theater 1940–1945 ⸺ U-47
Japanese Expansion 1875–1941 ⸺ U-48
World War II, Pacific Theater 1941–1945 ⸺ U-48–49
The World at War 1939–1945 ⸺ U-49
United States in the Postwar World ⸺ U-50–51
United States Interests in the Far East ⸺ U-52
The Korean Conflict 1950–1953 ⸺ U-53
The Vietnam Conflict 1961–1975 ⸺ U-53
Ethnic Distribution; Immigration 1981–1989 ⸺ U-54
Modern Urban Problems ⸺ U-55
Growth of the United States Economy ⸺ U-56–57
Alaska and Hawaii—Major Historical Events ⸺ U-58
The Fifty States: Population Distribution, Rank by Area, Rank by Population, Years of Admission to the Union ⸺ U-59
Population Characteristics ⸺ U-60
Development of Political Parties, Party Strength in Presidential Elections ⸺ U-61
Political Sectionalism, Presidential Electoral Vote by States and Parties ⸺ U-62–65
Presidents of the United States ⸺ U-65
Flags of American History ⸺ U-66–67
United States Political Map ⸺ U-68–69
Flags of States, Territories and Possessions ⸺ U-70–71
Index ⸺ U-72

ENTIRE CONTENTS © COPYRIGHT MCMXCVII BY HAMMOND INCORPORATED
All rights reserved. No part of this book may be reproduced or utilized in any form or by any means, electronic or mechanical, including photocopying, recording or by any information storage and retrieval system, without permission in writing from the Publisher.
LIBRARY OF CONGRESS CATALOG CARD NUMBER 96-49621
ISBN 0-8437-7440-1
PRINTED IN THE UNITED STATES OF AMERICA

Gazetteer of States, Territories and Possessions

State or Territory	Area (sq. mi.)†	Area (sq. km.)†	Population (1990)	Inhabitants per sq. mi. ††	Admitted to the Union	Settled at	Date
Alabama	52,423	135,775	4,040,587	79.6	Dec. 14, 1819	Mobile	1702
Alaska	656,424	1,700,139	550,043	1.0	Jan. 3, 1959	Sitka	1801
American Samoa	84	218	46,773	506.5	*Feb. 16, 1900	....	....
Arizona	114,006	295,276	3,665,228	32.3	Feb. 14, 1912	Tucson	1752
Arkansas	53,182	137,742	2,350,725	45.1	Jun. 15, 1836	Arkansas Post	1685
California	163,707	424,002	29,760,020	190.8	Sept. 9, 1850	San Diego	1769
Colorado	104,100	269,620	3,294,394	31.8	Aug. 1, 1876	Near Denver	1858
Connecticut	5,544	14,358	3,287,116	678.5	Jan. 9, 1788	Windsor	1635
Delaware	2,489	6,447	666,168	340.7	Dec. 7, 1787	Cape Henlopen	1627
District of Columbia	68	177	606,900	9,949.2	** 1790-1791	....	1790
Florida	65,758	170,313	12,937,926	239.6	Mar. 3, 1845	St. Augustine	1565
Georgia	59,441	153,953	6,478,216	111.8	Jan. 2, 1788	Savannah	1733
Guam	217	561	133,152	578.9	*Dec. 10, 1898	Agana	1668
Hawaii	10,932	28,313	1,108,229	172.5	Aug. 21, 1959	....	....
Idaho	83,574	216,456	1,006,749	12.2	July 3, 1890	Coeur d'Alene	1842
Illinois	57,918	150,007	11,430,602	205.6	Dec. 3, 1818	Kaskaskia	1720
Indiana	36,420	94,328	5,544,159	154.6	Dec. 11, 1816	Vincennes	1730
Iowa	56,276	145,754	2,776,755	49.7	Dec. 28, 1846	Burlington	1788
Kansas	82,282	213,110	2,477,574	30.3	Jan. 29, 1861	....	1831
Kentucky	40,411	104,665	3,685,296	92.8	June 1, 1792	Harrodsburg	1774
Louisiana	51,843	134,275	4,219,973	96.9	Apr. 30, 1812	Iberville	1699
Maine	35,387	91,653	1,227,928	39.8	Mar. 15, 1820	Bristol	1624
Maryland	12,407	32,135	4,781,468	489.1	Apr. 28, 1788	St. Mary's	1634
Massachusetts	10,555	27,337	6,016,425	767.6	Feb. 6, 1788	Plymouth	1620
Michigan	96,705	250,466	9,295,297	163.6	Jan. 26, 1837	Near Detroit	1650
Minnesota	86,943	225,182	4,375,099	54.9	May 11, 1858	St. Peter's River	1805
Mississippi	48,434	125,443	2,573,216	54.8	Dec. 10, 1817	Natchez	1716
Missouri	69,709	180,546	5,117,073	74.3	Aug. 10, 1821	St. Louis	1764
Montana	147,046	380,850	799,065	5.5	Nov. 8, 1889	....	1809
Nebraska	77,358	200,357	1,578,385	20.5	Mar. 1, 1867	Bellevue	1847
Nevada	110,567	286,368	1,201,833	10.9	Oct. 31, 1864	Genoa	1850
New Hampshire	9,351	24,219	1,109,252	123.7	June 21, 1788	Dover and Portsmouth	1623
New Jersey	8,722	22,590	7,730,188	1,041.9	Dec. 18, 1787	Bergen	1617
New Mexico	121,598	314,939	1,515,069	12.5	Jan. 6, 1912	Santa Fe	1605
New York	54,556	141,300	17,990,456	381.0	July 26, 1788	Manhattan Island	1614
North Carolina	53,821	139,397	6,628,637	136.1	Nov. 21, 1789	Albemarle	1650
North Dakota	70,704	183,123	638,800	9.3	Nov. 2, 1889	Pembina	1780
Northern Marianas	181	469	43,345	235.6	Apr. 2, 1947	....	....
Ohio	44,828	116,103	10,847,115	264.9	Mar. 1, 1803	Marietta	1788
Oklahoma	69,903	181,049	3,145,585	45.8	Nov. 16, 1907	....	1889
Oregon	98,386	254,819	2,842,321	29.6	Feb. 14, 1859	Astoria	1810
Pennsylvania	46,058	119,291	11,881,643	265.1	Dec. 12, 1787	Delaware River	1682
Puerto Rico	3,492	9,044	3,522,037	1,018.2	*Dec. 10, 1898	Caparra	1510
Rhode Island	1,545	4,002	1,003,464	960.2	May 29, 1790	Providence	1636
South Carolina	32,008	82,901	3,486,703	115.8	May 23, 1788	Port Royal	1670
South Dakota	77,121	199,743	696,004	9.2	Nov. 2, 1889	Sioux Falls	1856
Tennessee	42,146	109,158	4,877,185	118.3	June 1, 1796	Ft. Loudon	1757
Texas	268,601	695,676	16,986,510	64.9	Dec. 29, 1845	Matagorda Bay	1686
Utah	84,904	219,902	1,722,850	21.0	Jan. 4, 1896	Salt Lake City	1847
Vermont	9,615	24,903	562,758	60.8	Mar. 4, 1791	Ft. Dummer	1764
Virginia	42,777	110,792	6,187,358	156.2	June 26, 1788	Jamestown	1607
Virgin Islands	151	390	101,809	848.5	*Mar 31, 1917	St. Thomas I.	1657
Washington	71,302	184,672	4,866,692	73.1	Nov. 11, 1889	Astoria	1811
West Virginia	24,231	62,759	1,793,477	74.5	June 20, 1863	Wheeling	1774
Wisconsin	65,499	169,642	4,891,769	90.1	May 29, 1848	Green Bay	1670
Wyoming	97,818	253,349	453,588	4.7	July 10, 1890	Ft. Laramie	1834
United States	3,787,403	9,809,374	248,709,873	70.3	....	....	....
United States, Territories & Possessions	3,791,528	9,820,056	252,556,989	71.3	....	....	....

* Date of organization as Territory or acquisition by U.S.   ** Established under Acts of Congress   † Land and water.   †† Calculations based on land area.

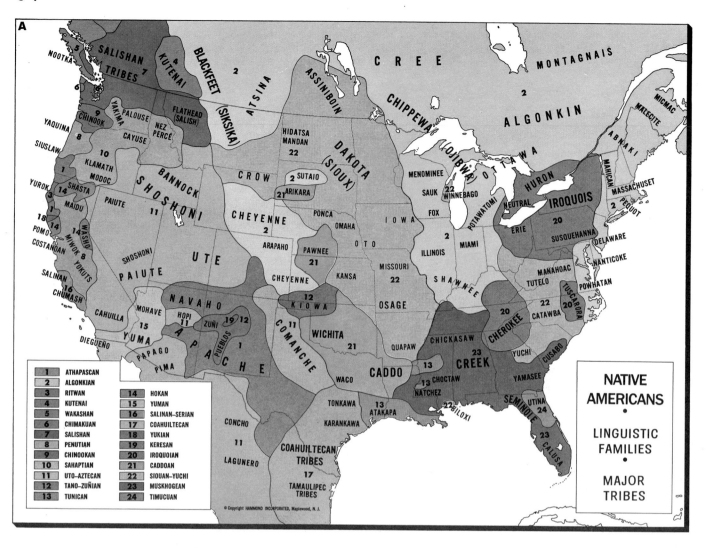

A

NATIVE
AMERICANS
•
LINGUISTIC
FAMILIES
•
MAJOR
TRIBES

1	ATHAPASCAN		
2	ALGONKIAN		
3	RITWAN	14	HOKAN
4	KUTENAI	15	YUMAN
5	WAKASHAN	16	SALINAN–SERIAN
6	CHIMAKUAN	17	COAHUILTECAN
7	SALISHAN	18	YUKIAN
8	PENUTIAN	19	KERESAN
9	CHINOOKAN	20	IROQUOIAN
10	SAHAPTIAN	21	CADDOAN
11	UTO–AZTECAN	22	SIOUAN–YUCHI
12	TANO–ZUÑIAN	23	MUSKHOGEAN
13	TUNICAN	24	TIMUCUAN

© Copyright HAMMOND INCORPORATED, Maplewood, N. J.

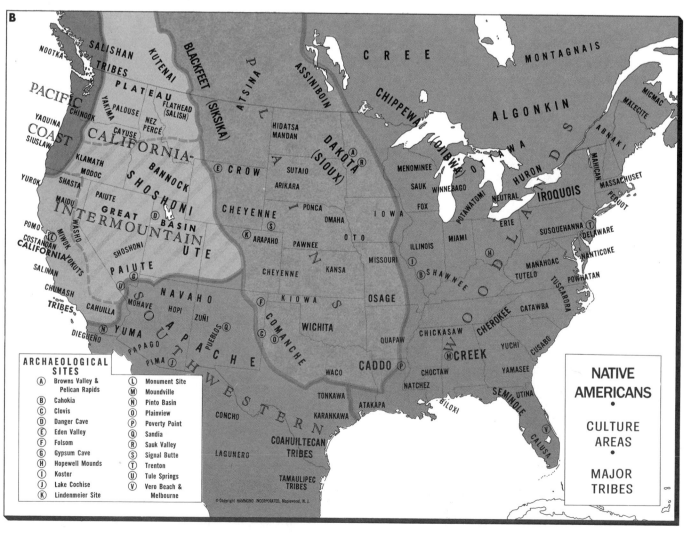

B

NATIVE
AMERICANS
•
CULTURE
AREAS
•
MAJOR
TRIBES

ARCHAEOLOGICAL
SITES

A	Browns Valley & Pelican Rapids	L	Monument Site
B	Cahokia	M	Moundville
C	Clovis	N	Pinto Basin
D	Danger Cave	O	Plainview
E	Eden Valley	P	Poverty Point
F	Folsom	Q	Sandia
G	Gypsum Cave	R	Sauk Valley
H	Hopewell Mounds	S	Signal Butte
I	Koster	T	Trenton
J	Lake Cochise	U	Tule Springs
K	Lindenmeier Site	V	Vero Beach & Melbourne

© Copyright HAMMOND INCORPORATED, Maplewood, N. J.

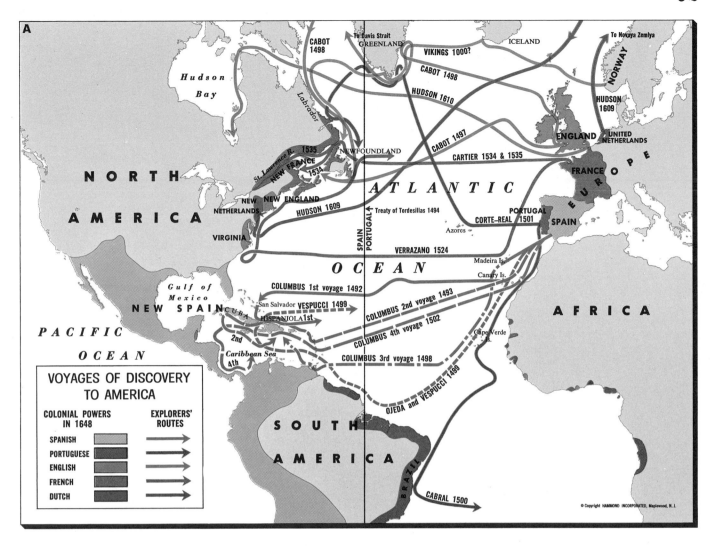

A

VOYAGES OF DISCOVERY TO AMERICA

COLONIAL POWERS IN 1648 — EXPLORERS' ROUTES

SPANISH
PORTUGUESE
ENGLISH
FRENCH
DUTCH

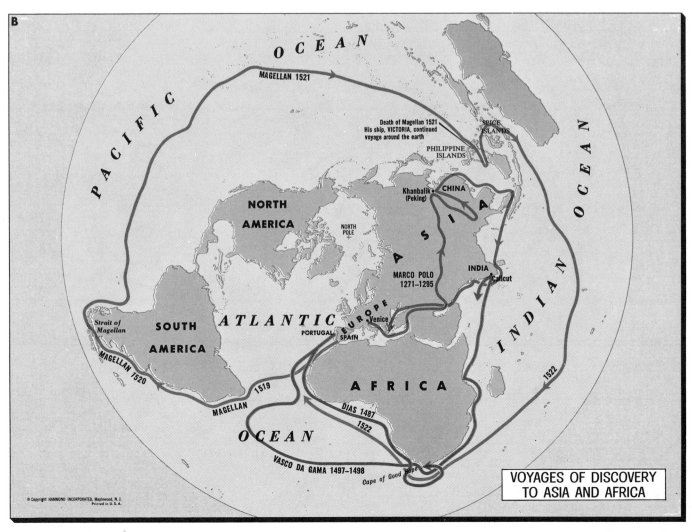

B

VOYAGES OF DISCOVERY TO ASIA AND AFRICA

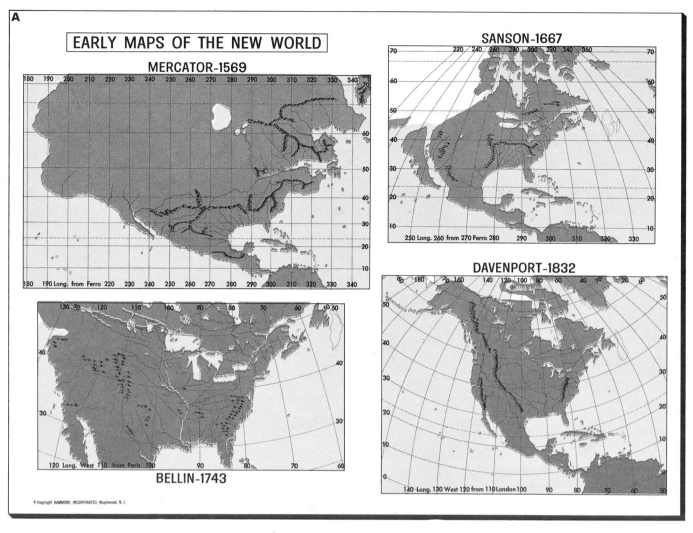

A

EARLY MAPS OF THE NEW WORLD

MERCATOR-1569

SANSON-1667

DAVENPORT-1832

BELLIN-1743

© Copyright HAMMOND INCORPORATED, Maplewood, N.J.

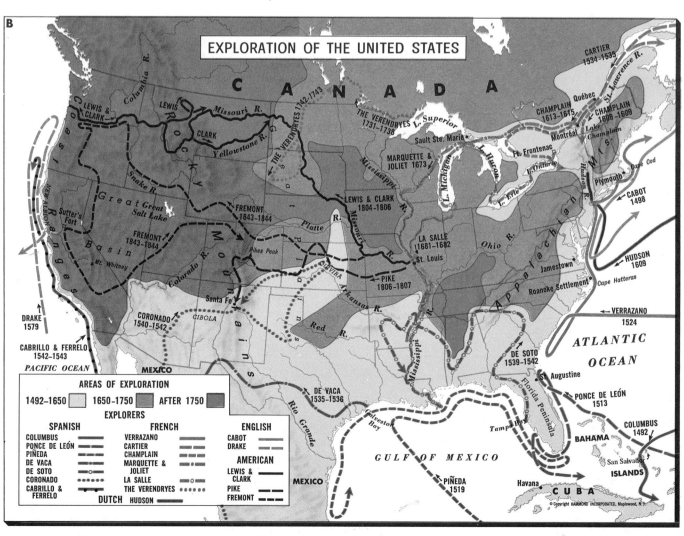

B

EXPLORATION OF THE UNITED STATES

AREAS OF EXPLORATION

1492–1650 1650–1750 AFTER 1750

EXPLORERS

SPANISH	FRENCH	ENGLISH
COLUMBUS	VERRAZANO	CABOT
PONCE DE LEÓN	CARTIER	DRAKE
PIÑEDA	CHAMPLAIN	**AMERICAN**
DE VACA	MARQUETTE & JOLIET	LEWIS & CLARK
DE SOTO	LA SALLE	PIKE
CORONADO	THE VERENDRYES	FREMONT
CABRILLO & FERRELO		

DUTCH HUDSON

© Copyright HAMMOND INCORPORATED, Maplewood, N.J.

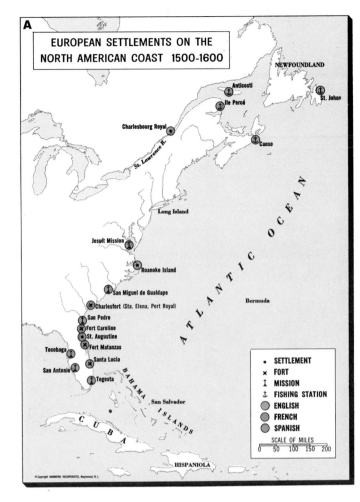

A

EUROPEAN SETTLEMENTS ON THE NORTH AMERICAN COAST 1500-1600

NEWFOUNDLAND

Anticosti
Ile Percé
St. Johns

Charlesbourg Royal

St. Lawrence R.

Canso

Long Island

Jesuit Mission

Roanoke Island

San Miguel de Gualdape

Charlesfort (Sta. Elena, Port Royal)
San Pedro
Fort Caroline
St. Augustine
Fort Matanzas
Tocobaga
Santa Lucía
San Antonio
Tegesta

ATLANTIC OCEAN

Bermuda

BAHAMA ISLANDS

San Salvador

CUBA

HISPANIOLA

• SETTLEMENT
× FORT
⊥ MISSION
↓ FISHING STATION
⬤ ENGLISH
⬤ FRENCH
⬤ SPANISH

SCALE OF MILES
0 50 100 150 200

© Copyright HAMMOND INCORPORATED, Maplewood, N.J.

B

EUROPEAN POWERS IN THE NEW WORLD 1682

HUDSON BAY

HUDSON'S BAY COMPANY

NEWFOUND-LAND

NEW FRANCE

ACADIA

Great Lakes
St. Lawrence R.

NEW ENGLAND

ENGLISH COLONIES

VIRGINIA

LOUISIANA

Mississippi

CAROLINA

FLORIDA

GULF OF MEXICO

CUBA

NEW SPAIN

CARIBBEAN SEA

PACIFIC OCEAN

ATLANTIC OCEAN

NEW GRANADA

ENGLISH
FRENCH
SPANISH

SCALE OF MILES
0 200 400 600

© Copyright HAMMOND INCORPORATED, Maplewood, N.J.

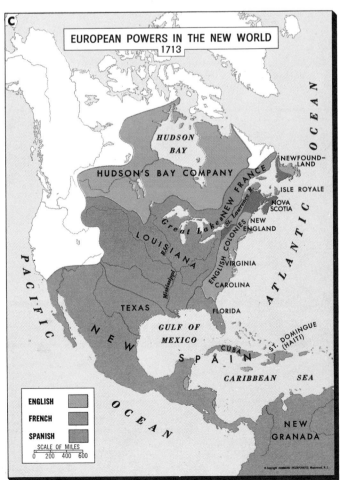

C

EUROPEAN POWERS IN THE NEW WORLD 1713

HUDSON BAY

HUDSON'S BAY COMPANY

NEWFOUND-LAND

NEW FRANCE

ISLE ROYALE

NOVA SCOTIA

Great Lakes
St. Lawrence R.

NEW ENGLAND

ENGLISH COLONIES

VIRGINIA

LOUISIANA

Mississippi

CAROLINA

TEXAS

FLORIDA

GULF OF MEXICO

CUBA

NEW SPAIN

ST. DOMINGUE (HAITI)

CARIBBEAN SEA

PACIFIC OCEAN

ATLANTIC OCEAN

NEW GRANADA

ENGLISH
FRENCH
SPANISH

SCALE OF MILES
0 200 400 600

© Copyright HAMMOND INCORPORATED, Maplewood, N.J.

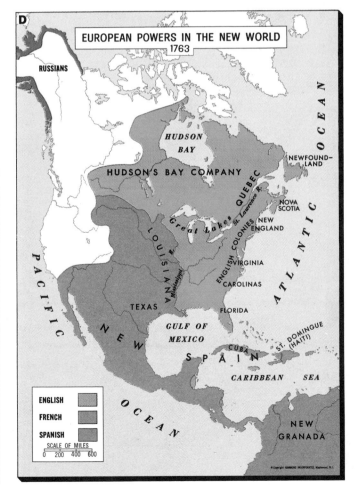

D

EUROPEAN POWERS IN THE NEW WORLD 1763

RUSSIANS

HUDSON BAY

HUDSON'S BAY COMPANY

NEWFOUND-LAND

QUEBEC

NOVA SCOTIA

Great Lakes
St. Lawrence R.

NEW ENGLAND

ENGLISH COLONIES

VIRGINIA

LOUISIANA

Mississippi

CAROLINAS

TEXAS

FLORIDA

GULF OF MEXICO

CUBA

NEW SPAIN

ST. DOMINGUE (HAITI)

CARIBBEAN SEA

PACIFIC OCEAN

ATLANTIC OCEAN

NEW GRANADA

ENGLISH
FRENCH
SPANISH

SCALE OF MILES
0 200 400 600

© Copyright HAMMOND INCORPORATED, Maplewood, N.J.

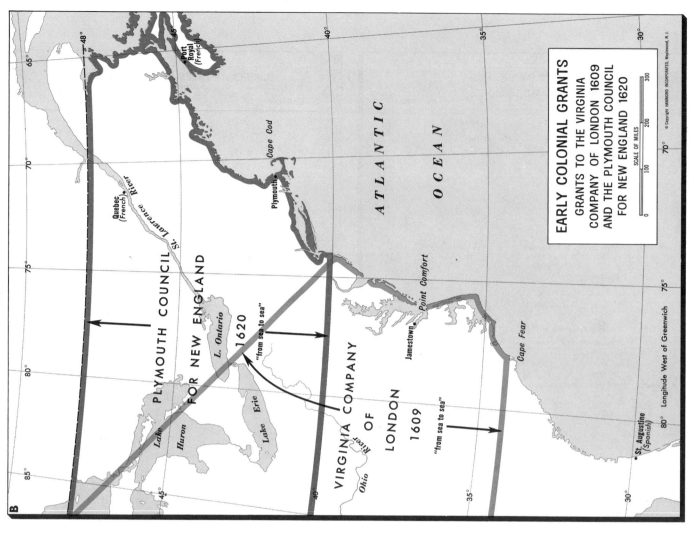

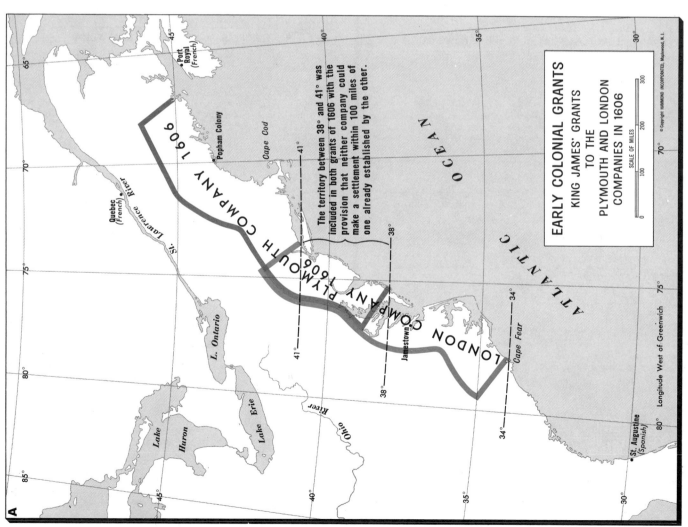

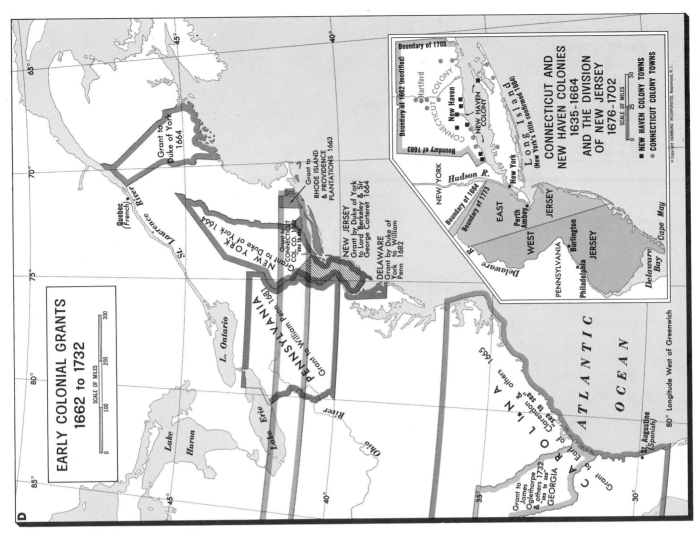

EARLY COLONIAL GRANTS 1662 to 1732

SCALE OF MILES
0 100 200 300

CONNECTICUT AND NEW HAVEN COLONIES 1635-1664 AND THE DIVISION OF NEW JERSEY 1676-1702

SCALE OF MILES
0 25 50

■ NEW HAVEN COLONY TOWNS
● CONNECTICUT COLONY TOWNS

© Copyright HAMMOND INCORPORATED, Maplewood, N.J.

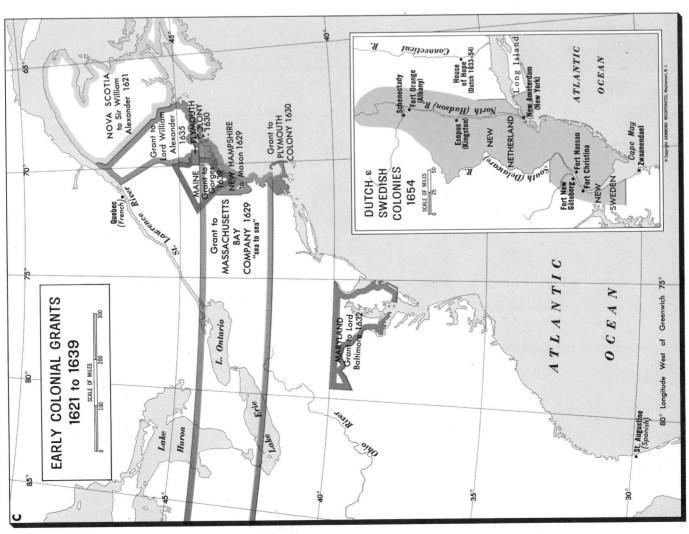

EARLY COLONIAL GRANTS 1621 to 1639

SCALE OF MILES
0 100 200 300

DUTCH & SWEDISH COLONIES 1654

SCALE OF MILES
0 25 50

© Copyright HAMMOND INCORPORATED, Maplewood, N.J.

A

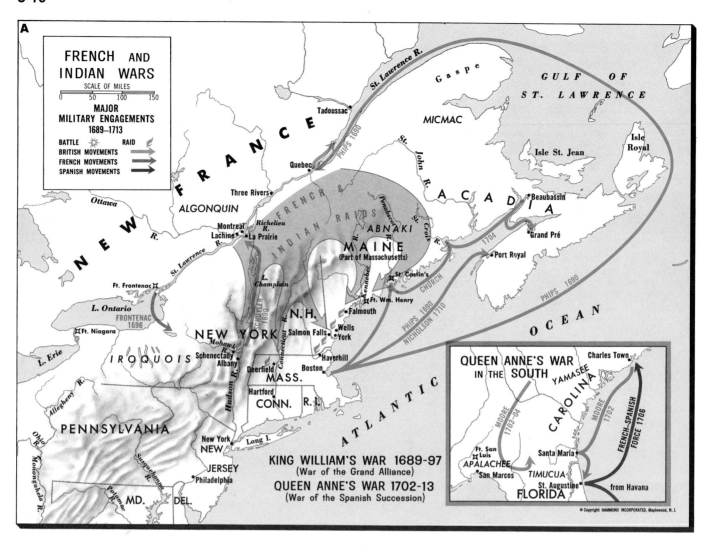

FRENCH AND INDIAN WARS

SCALE OF MILES
0   50   100   150

MAJOR MILITARY ENGAGEMENTS 1689–1713

BATTLE   RAID
BRITISH MOVEMENTS
FRENCH MOVEMENTS
SPANISH MOVEMENTS

KING WILLIAM'S WAR 1689-97
(War of the Grand Alliance)
QUEEN ANNE'S WAR 1702-13
(War of the Spanish Succession)

QUEEN ANNE'S WAR IN THE SOUTH

© Copyright HAMMOND INCORPORATED, Maplewood, N.J.

B

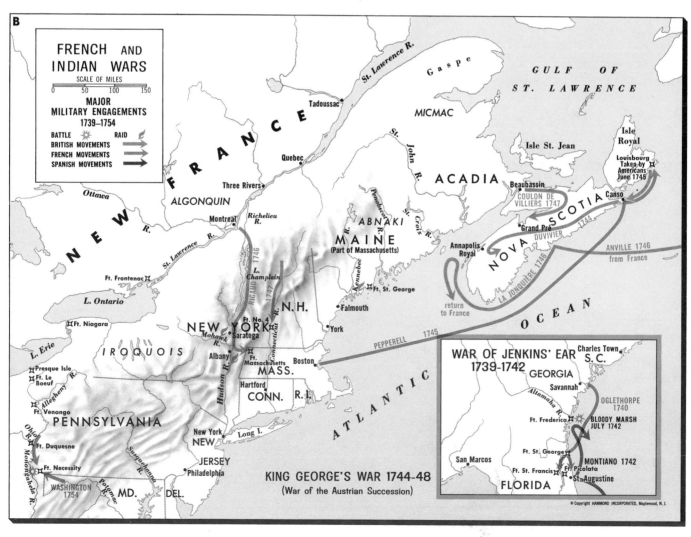

FRENCH AND INDIAN WARS

SCALE OF MILES
0   50   100   150

MAJOR MILITARY ENGAGEMENTS 1739–1754

BATTLE   RAID
BRITISH MOVEMENTS
FRENCH MOVEMENTS
SPANISH MOVEMENTS

KING GEORGE'S WAR 1744-48
(War of the Austrian Succession)

WAR OF JENKINS' EAR 1739-1742

© Copyright HAMMOND INCORPORATED, Maplewood, N.J.

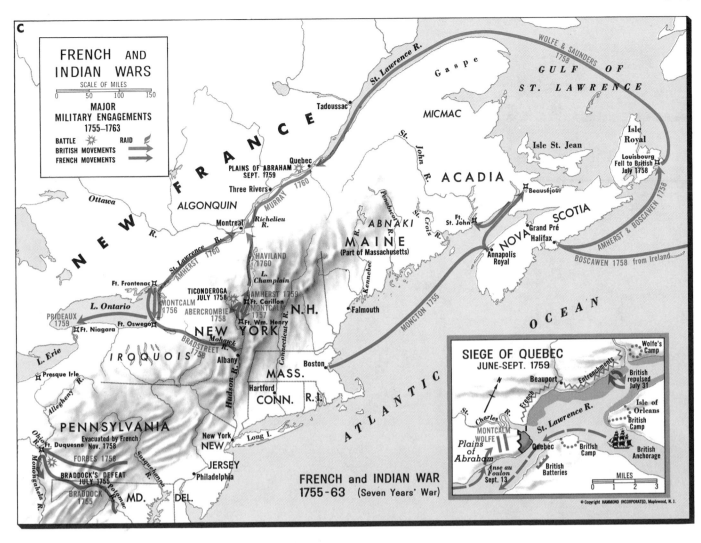

FRENCH AND INDIAN WARS

SCALE OF MILES
0 50 100 150

MAJOR MILITARY ENGAGEMENTS 1755–1763

BATTLE ✳   RAID ⚔
BRITISH MOVEMENTS →
FRENCH MOVEMENTS →

FRENCH and INDIAN WAR
1755-63 (Seven Years' War)

SIEGE OF QUEBEC
JUNE–SEPT. 1759

Wolfe's Camp
British repulsed July 31
Isle of Orleans
British Camp
Beauport
Entrenchments
St. Lawrence R.
MONTCALM
WOLFE
Plains of Abraham
Quebec
British Camp
British Anchorage
Anse au Foulon Sept. 13
British Batteries

MILES
0 1 2 3

© Copyright HAMMOND INCORPORATED, Maplewood, N.J.

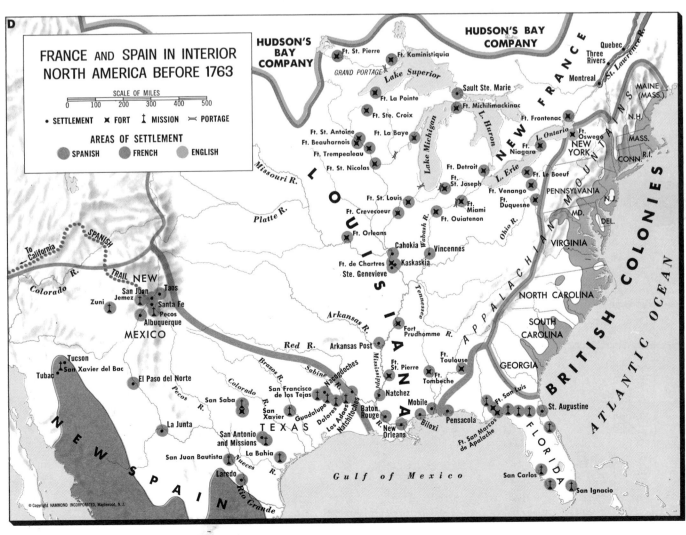

FRANCE AND SPAIN IN INTERIOR NORTH AMERICA BEFORE 1763

SCALE OF MILES
0 100 200 300 400 500

● SETTLEMENT   ✕ FORT   ☩ MISSION   ⋈ PORTAGE

AREAS OF SETTLEMENT
SPANISH   FRENCH   ENGLISH

© Copyright HAMMOND INCORPORATED, Maplewood, N.J.

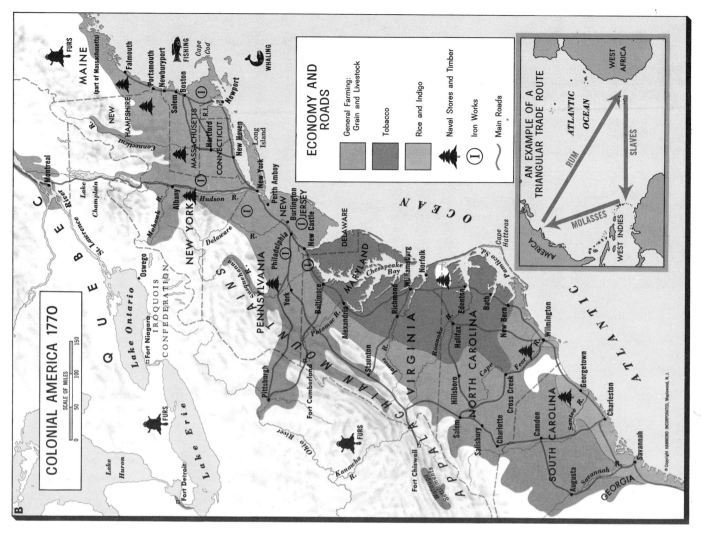

COLONIAL AMERICA 1770

SCALE OF MILES
0   50   100   150

ECONOMY AND ROADS

General Farming: Grain and Livestock

Tobacco

Rice and Indigo

Naval Stores and Timber

Ⓘ Iron Works

Main Roads

AN EXAMPLE OF A TRIANGULAR TRADE ROUTE

ATLANTIC OCEAN

WEST AFRICA

RUM

SLAVES

MOLASSES

WEST INDIES

AMERICA

© Copyright HAMMOND INCORPORATED, Maplewood, N.J.

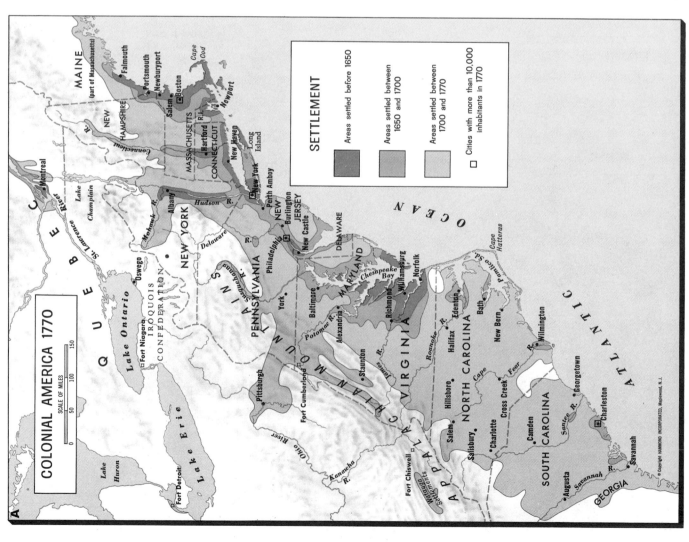

COLONIAL AMERICA 1770

SCALE OF MILES
0   50   100   150

SETTLEMENT

Areas settled before 1650

Areas settled between 1650 and 1700

Areas settled between 1700 and 1770

□ Cities with more than 10,000 inhabitants in 1770

© Copyright HAMMOND INCORPORATED, Maplewood, N.J.

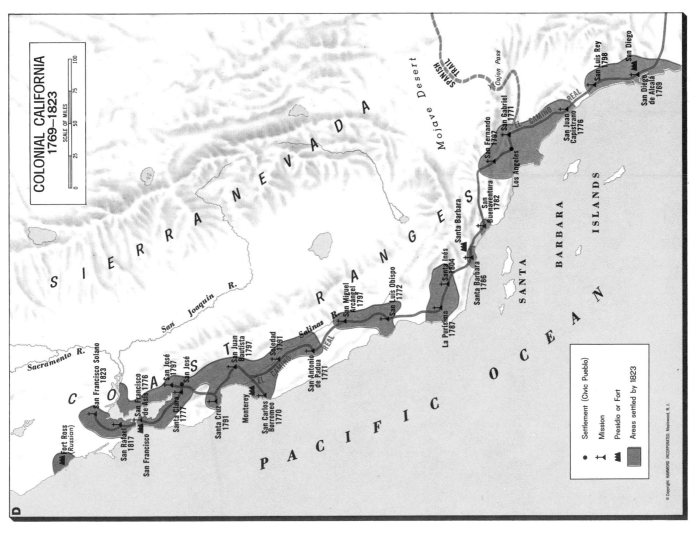

COLONIAL CALIFORNIA 1769–1823

SCALE OF MILES
0   25   50   75   100

SIERRA NEVADA

COAST RANGES

Sacramento R.
San Joaquin R.
Salinas R.

Mojave Desert

SPANISH TRAIL
Cajon Pass

Fort Ross (Russian)

San Rafael 1817
San Francisco Solano 1823
San Francisco de Asis 1776
San Francisco
San José 1797
Santa Clara 1777
San José
Santa Cruz 1791
Monterey
San Carlos Borromeo 1770
San Juan Bautista 1797
Soledad 1791
San Antonio de Padua 1771
San Miguel Arcángel 1797
San Luis Obispo 1772
La Purísima 1787
Santa Inés 1804
Santa Barbara 1786
Santa Barbara
San Buenaventura 1782
San Fernando 1797
San Gabriel 1771
Los Angeles
San Juan Capistrano 1776
San Luis Rey 1798
San Diego
San Diego de Alcalá 1769

EL CAMINO REAL

SANTA BARBARA ISLANDS

PACIFIC OCEAN

Legend:
- ● Settlement (Civic Pueblo)
- ✝ Mission
- ▲ Presidio or Fort
- ▨ Areas settled by 1823

© Copyright HAMMOND INCORPORATED, Maplewood, N.J.

D

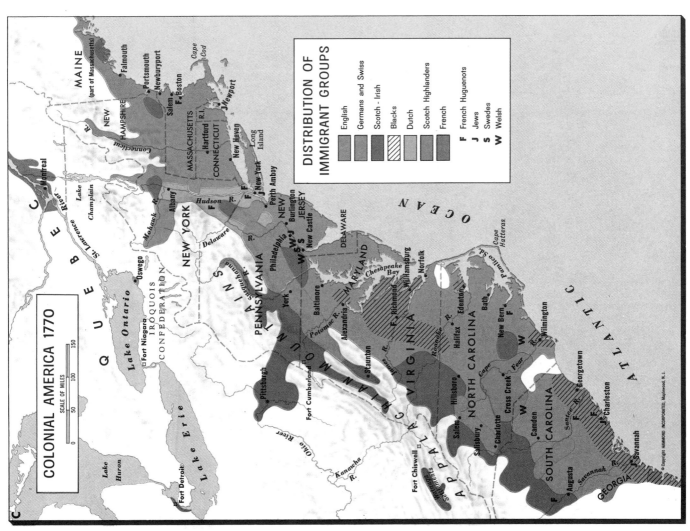

COLONIAL AMERICA 1770

SCALE OF MILES
0   50   100   150

QUEBEC

Lake Huron
Lake Erie
Lake Ontario
Lake Champlain

Fort Detroit
Fort Niagara
Oswego
Montreal
St. Lawrence River

IROQUOIS CONFEDERATION

Ohio River
Kanawha R.

Fort Chiswell
Fort Cumberland
Pittsburgh

MAINE (part of Massachusetts)

NEW HAMPSHIRE
NEW YORK
MASSACHUSETTS
CONNECTICUT
R.I.
NEW JERSEY
PENNSYLVANIA
MARYLAND
DELAWARE
VIRGINIA
NORTH CAROLINA
SOUTH CAROLINA
GEORGIA

APPALACHIAN MOUNTAINS

Falmouth
Portsmouth
Newburyport
Salem
Boston
Newport
New Haven
Hartford
Long Island
New York
Perth Amboy
Albany
Burlington
New Castle
Philadelphia
York
Baltimore
Alexandria
Richmond
Williamsburg
Norfolk
Edenton
Bath
New Bern
Halifax
Hillsboro
Wilmington
Salem
Salisbury
Charlotte
Cross Creek
Camden
Georgetown
Charleston
Augusta
Savannah
Staunton

Cape Cod
Cape Hatteras
Cape Fear
Pamlico Sd.
Chesapeake Bay
Hudson R.
Mohawk R.
Delaware R.
Susquehanna R.
Potomac R.
Roanoke R.
Cape Fear R.
Santee R.
Savannah R.

ATLANTIC OCEAN

DISTRIBUTION OF IMMIGRANT GROUPS

- English
- Germans and Swiss
- Scotch-Irish
- Blacks
- Dutch
- Scotch Highlanders
- French
- **F** French Huguenots
- **J** Jews
- **S** Swedes
- **W** Welsh

© Copyright HAMMOND INCORPORATED, Maplewood, N.J.

C

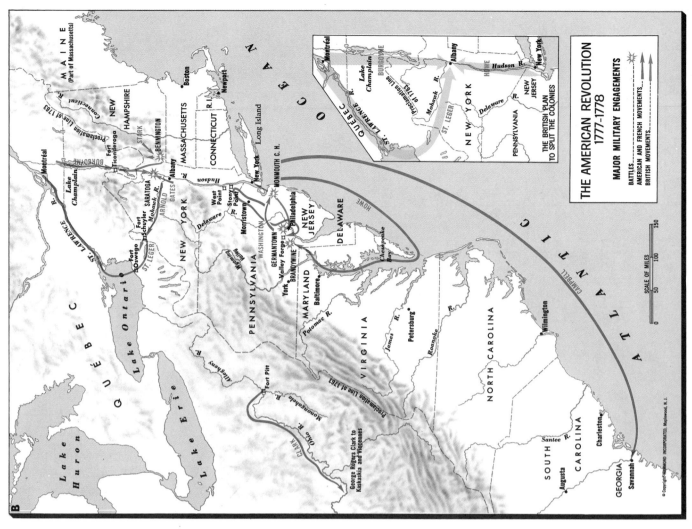

THE AMERICAN REVOLUTION
1777-1778

MAJOR MILITARY ENGAGEMENTS

BATTLES
AMERICAN AND FRENCH MOVEMENTS
BRITISH MOVEMENTS

THE BRITISH PLAN
TO SPLIT THE COLONIES

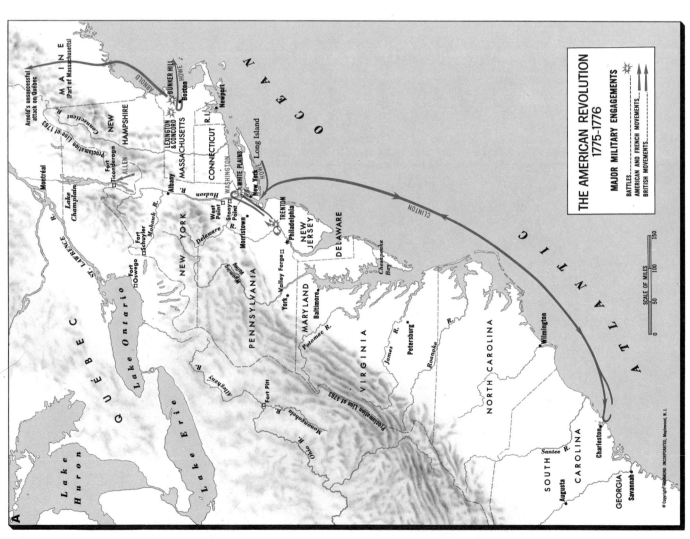

THE AMERICAN REVOLUTION
1775-1776

MAJOR MILITARY ENGAGEMENTS

BATTLES
AMERICAN AND FRENCH MOVEMENTS
BRITISH MOVEMENTS

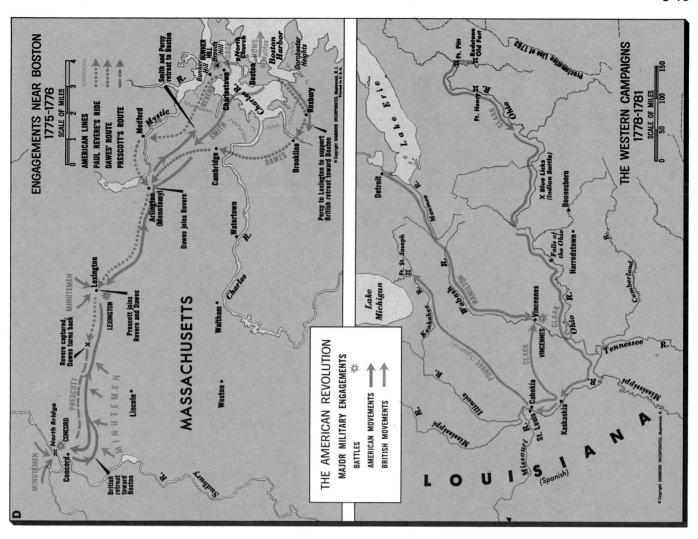

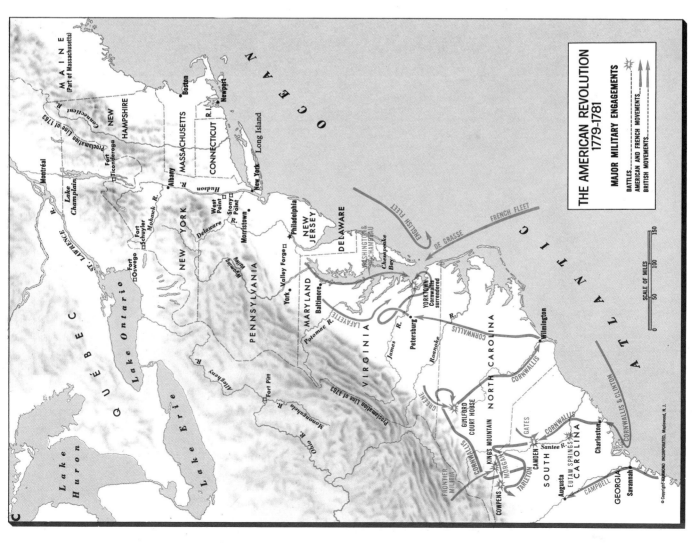

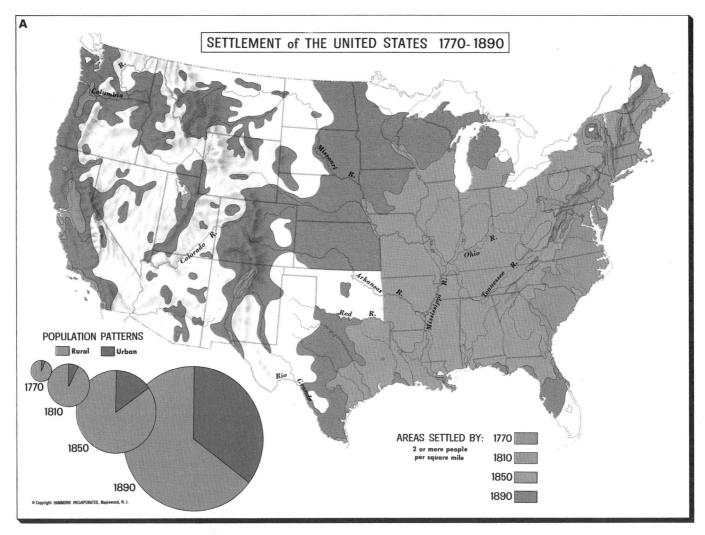

A

SETTLEMENT of THE UNITED STATES 1770-1890

POPULATION PATTERNS

Rural   Urban

1770
1810
1850
1890

AREAS SETTLED BY: 1770
2 or more people   1810
per square mile   1850
                      1890

© Copyright HAMMOND INCORPORATED, Maplewood, N. J.

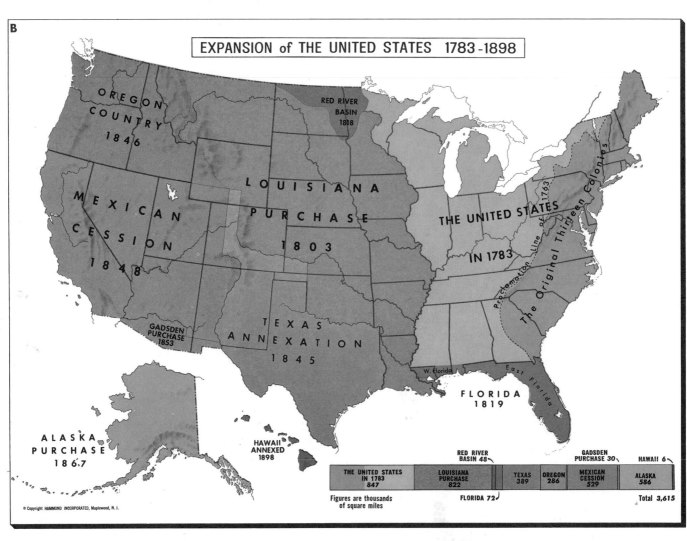

B

EXPANSION of THE UNITED STATES 1783-1898

OREGON COUNTRY 1846

RED RIVER BASIN 1818

MEXICAN CESSION 1848

LOUISIANA PURCHASE 1803

THE UNITED STATES IN 1783

Proclamation Line of 1763

The Original Thirteen Colonies

GADSDEN PURCHASE 1853

TEXAS ANNEXATION 1845

W. Florida   East Florida

FLORIDA 1819

ALASKA PURCHASE 1867

HAWAII ANNEXED 1898

THE UNITED STATES IN 1783 847	LOUISIANA PURCHASE 822	RED RIVER BASIN 48	TEXAS 389	OREGON 286	GADSDEN PURCHASE 30	MEXICAN CESSION 529	HAWAII 6	ALASKA 586

Figures are thousands of square miles   FLORIDA 72   Total 3,615

© Copyright HAMMOND INCORPORATED, Maplewood, N. J.

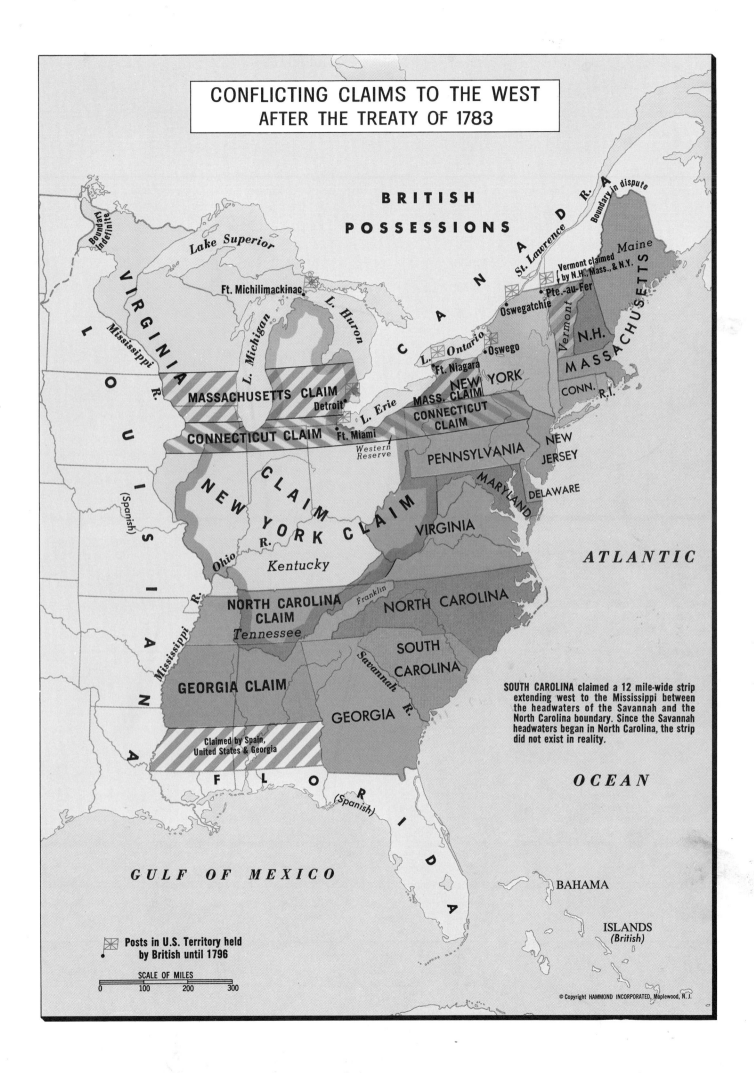

CONFLICTING CLAIMS TO THE WEST
AFTER THE TREATY OF 1783

BRITISH
POSSESSIONS

C A N A D A

Boundary in dispute

Boundary Indefinite

Lake Superior

St. Lawrence R.

Maine

Vermont claimed by N.H., Mass., & N.Y.

VIRGINIA

Ft. Michilimackinac

L. Huron

L. Michigan

Oswegatchie

Pte.-au-Fer

L O U I S I A N A

Mississippi R.

MASSACHUSETTS CLAIM

Detroit

L. Ontario

Oswego

Vermont

N.H.

MASSACHUSETTS

Ft. Niagara

NEW YORK

CONN.

R.I.

(Spanish)

CONNECTICUT CLAIM

Ft. Miami

L. Erie

MASS. CLAIM

CONNECTICUT CLAIM

Western Reserve

PENNSYLVANIA

NEW JERSEY

MARYLAND

DELAWARE

N E W   Y O R K   C L A I M

Ohio R.

Kentucky

VIRGINIA

ATLANTIC

Mississippi R.

NORTH CAROLINA CLAIM

Tennessee

Franklin

NORTH CAROLINA

SOUTH CAROLINA

Savannah R.

GEORGIA CLAIM

GEORGIA

SOUTH CAROLINA claimed a 12 mile-wide strip extending west to the Mississippi between the headwaters of the Savannah and the North Carolina boundary. Since the Savannah headwaters began in North Carolina, the strip did not exist in reality.

Claimed by Spain, United States & Georgia

F L O R I D A

(Spanish)

OCEAN

GULF OF MEXICO

BAHAMA

ISLANDS (British)

⊞• Posts in U.S. Territory held by British until 1796

SCALE OF MILES

0   100   200   300

© Copyright HAMMOND INCORPORATED, Maplewood, N.J.

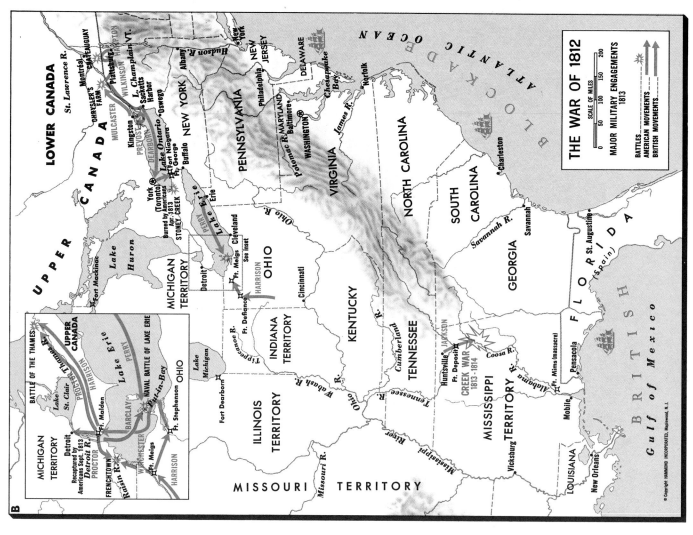

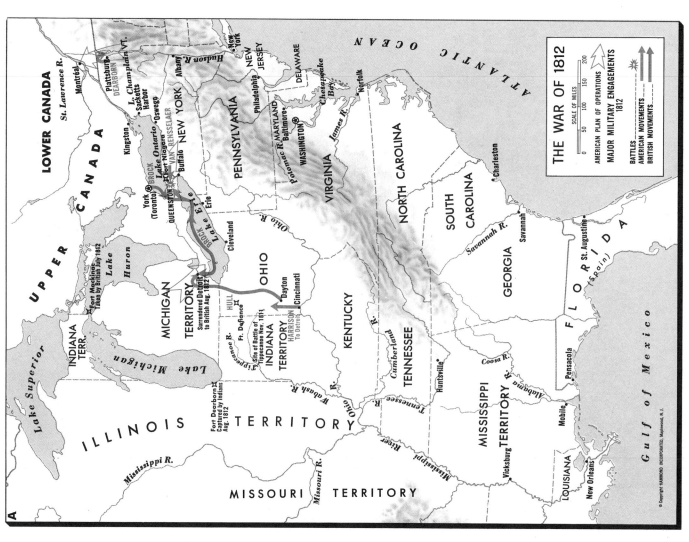

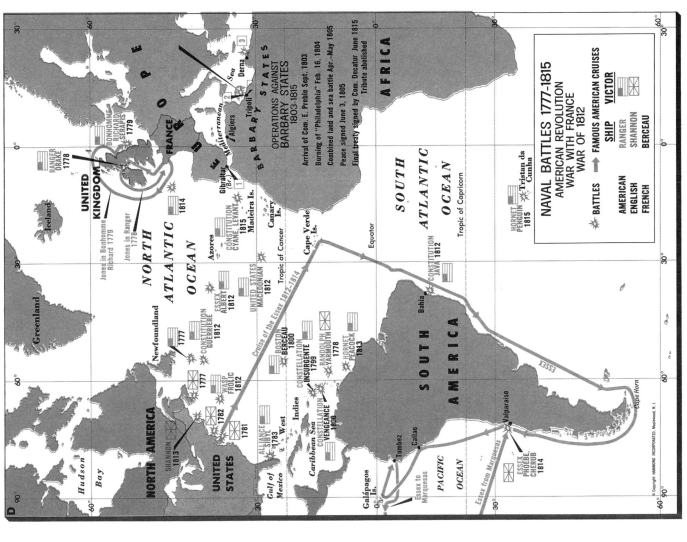

NAVAL BATTLES 1777-1815
AMERICAN REVOLUTION
WAR WITH FRANCE
WAR OF 1812

OPERATIONS AGAINST BARBARY STATES 1803-1815

Arrival of Com. E. Preble Sept. 1803
Burning of "Philadelphia" Feb. 16, 1804
Combined land and sea battle Apr.–May 1805
Peace signed June 3, 1805
Final treaty signed by Com. Decatur June 1815
Tribute abolished

SHIP	VICTOR
RANGER	
SHANNON	
BERCEAU	

❊ BATTLES → FAMOUS AMERICAN CRUISES

AMERICAN
ENGLISH
FRENCH

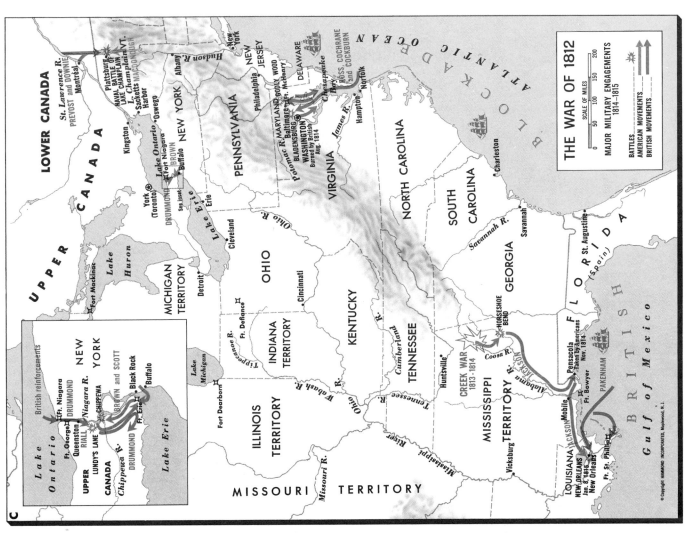

THE WAR OF 1812

SCALE OF MILES
0 50 100 150 200

MAJOR MILITARY ENGAGEMENTS
1814-1815

❊ BATTLES
⇒ AMERICAN MOVEMENTS
⇒ BRITISH MOVEMENTS

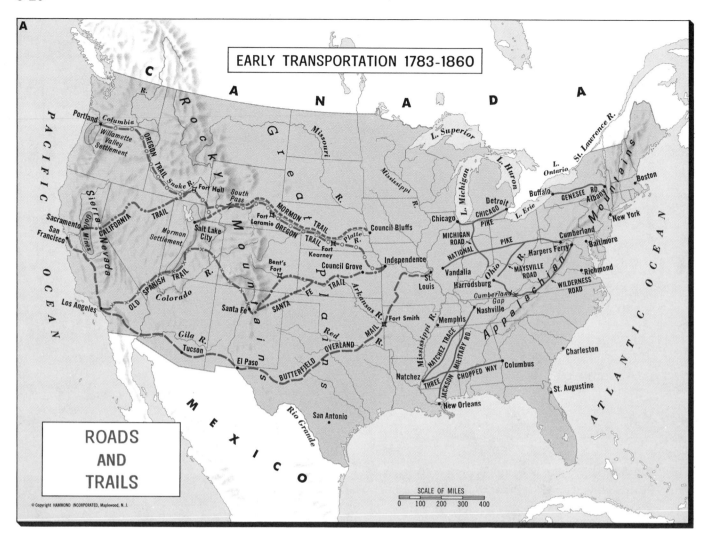

EARLY TRANSPORTATION 1783-1860

ROADS AND TRAILS

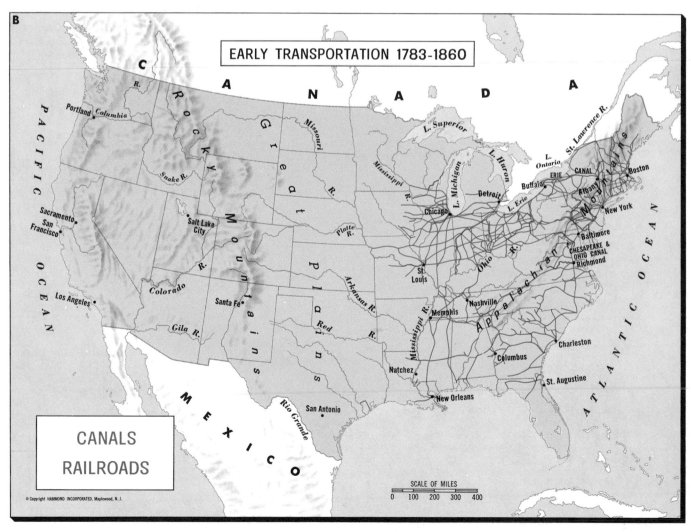

EARLY TRANSPORTATION 1783-1860

CANALS RAILROADS

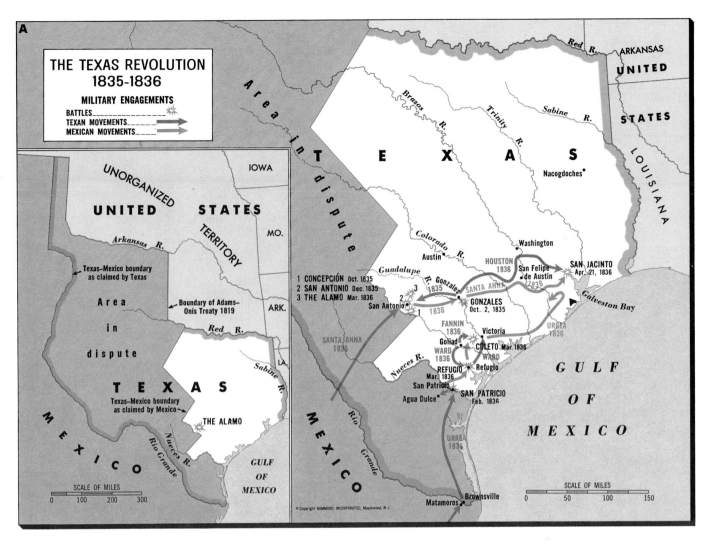

THE TEXAS REVOLUTION 1835-1836

MILITARY ENGAGEMENTS
- BATTLES
- TEXAN MOVEMENTS
- MEXICAN MOVEMENTS

1 CONCEPCIÓN Oct. 1835
2 SAN ANTONIO Dec. 1835
3 THE ALAMO Mar. 1836

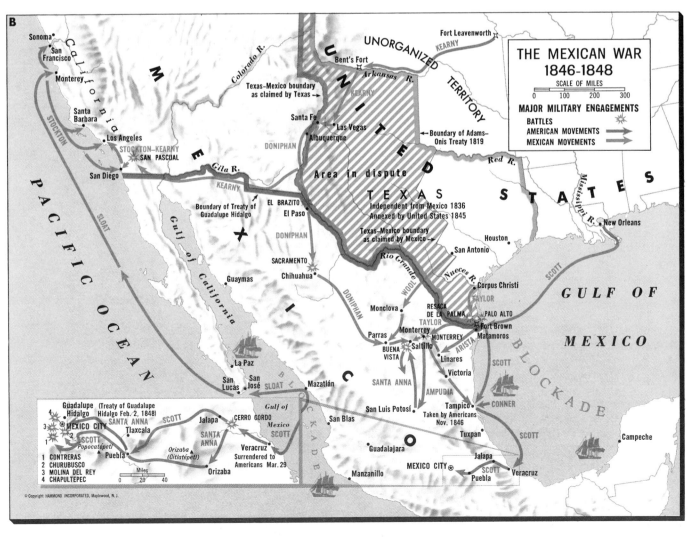

THE MEXICAN WAR 1846-1848

SCALE OF MILES
0   100   200   300

MAJOR MILITARY ENGAGEMENTS
- BATTLES
- AMERICAN MOVEMENTS
- MEXICAN MOVEMENTS

TEXAS
Independent from Mexico 1836
Annexed by United States 1845

1 CONTRERAS
2 CHURUBUSCO
3 MOLINA DEL REY
4 CHAPULTEPEC

Guadalupe Hidalgo (Treaty of Guadalupe Hidalgo Feb. 2, 1848)

Veracruz Surrendered to Americans Mar. 29

Tampico Taken by Americans Nov. 1846

© Copyright HAMMOND INCORPORATED, Maplewood, N.J.

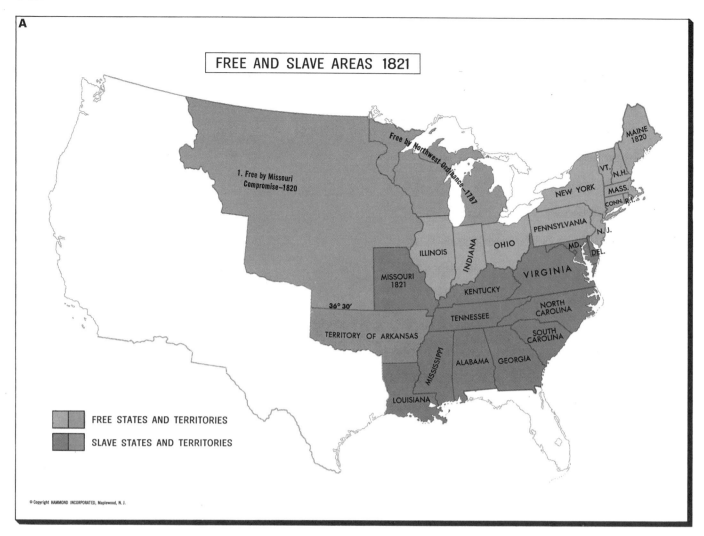

FREE AND SLAVE AREAS 1821

1. Free by Missouri Compromise—1820

Free by Northwest Ordinance—1787

MAINE 1820

VT. N.H.

NEW YORK MASS. CONN. R.I.

PENNSYLVANIA N.J.

ILLINOIS INDIANA OHIO MD. DEL.

MISSOURI 1821

VIRGINIA

KENTUCKY

36° 30'

TENNESSEE NORTH CAROLINA

TERRITORY OF ARKANSAS SOUTH CAROLINA

MISSISSIPPI ALABAMA GEORGIA

LOUISIANA

FREE STATES AND TERRITORIES

SLAVE STATES AND TERRITORIES

© Copyright HAMMOND INCORPORATED, Maplewood, N. J.

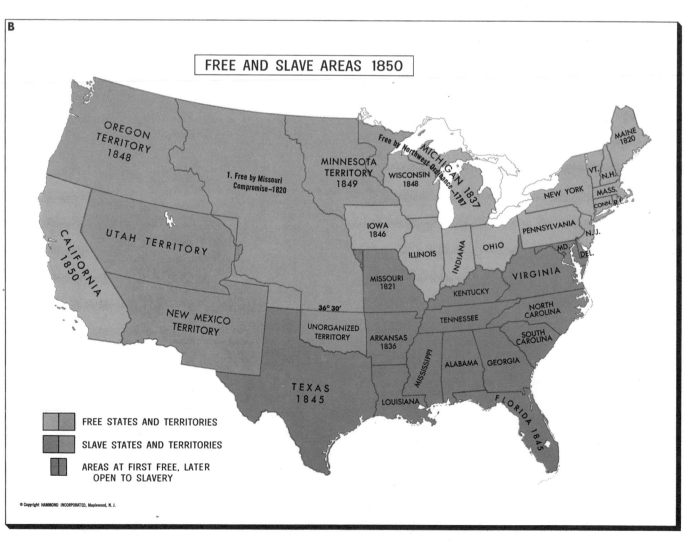

FREE AND SLAVE AREAS 1850

OREGON TERRITORY 1848

1. Free by Missouri Compromise—1820

MINNESOTA TERRITORY 1849

Free by Northwest Ordinance—1787

MICHIGAN 1837

WISCONSIN 1848

MAINE 1820

VT. N.H.

NEW YORK MASS. CONN. R.I.

UTAH TERRITORY

CALIFORNIA 1850

IOWA 1846

PENNSYLVANIA N.J.

ILLINOIS INDIANA OHIO MD. DEL.

MISSOURI 1821

VIRGINIA

KENTUCKY

NEW MEXICO TERRITORY

36° 30'

UNORGANIZED TERRITORY

ARKANSAS 1836

TENNESSEE NORTH CAROLINA

SOUTH CAROLINA

MISSISSIPPI ALABAMA GEORGIA

TEXAS 1845

LOUISIANA

FLORIDA 1845

FREE STATES AND TERRITORIES

SLAVE STATES AND TERRITORIES

AREAS AT FIRST FREE, LATER OPEN TO SLAVERY

© Copyright HAMMOND INCORPORATED, Maplewood, N. J.

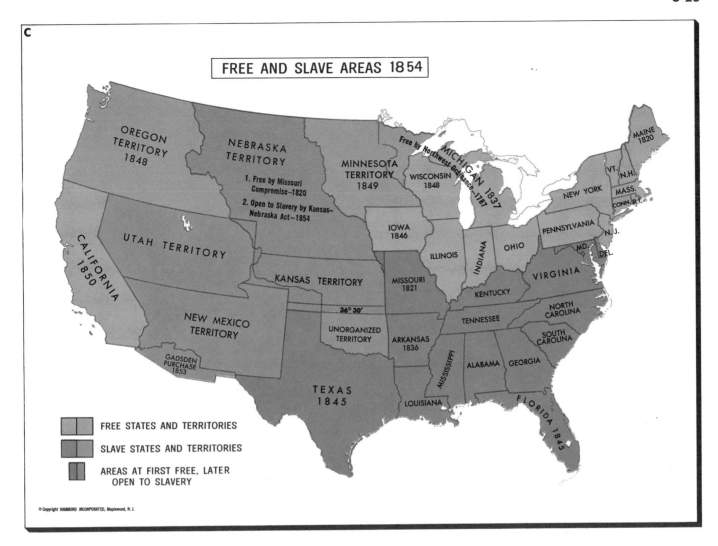

C

FREE AND SLAVE AREAS 1854

OREGON TERRITORY 1848

NEBRASKA TERRITORY
1. Free by Missouri Compromise–1820
2. Open to Slavery by Kansas–Nebraska Act–1854

MINNESOTA TERRITORY 1849

WISCONSIN 1848

Free by Northwest Ordinance–1787

MICHIGAN 1837

MAINE 1820

VT. N.H.

NEW YORK

MASS.
CONN. R.I.

UTAH TERRITORY

IOWA 1846

ILLINOIS

INDIANA

OHIO

PENNSYLVANIA

N.J.

CALIFORNIA 1850

KANSAS TERRITORY

MISSOURI 1821

KENTUCKY

VIRGINIA

MD.

DEL.

NEW MEXICO TERRITORY

36° 30'

UNORGANIZED TERRITORY

TENNESSEE

NORTH CAROLINA

ARKANSAS 1836

SOUTH CAROLINA

GADSDEN PURCHASE 1853

MISSISSIPPI

ALABAMA

GEORGIA

TEXAS 1845

LOUISIANA

FLORIDA 1845

FREE STATES AND TERRITORIES

SLAVE STATES AND TERRITORIES

AREAS AT FIRST FREE, LATER OPEN TO SLAVERY

D

FREE AND SLAVE AREAS 1861
at the outbreak of the Civil War

WASHINGTON TERRITORY

OREGON 1859

DAKOTA TERRITORY

MINNESOTA 1858

MICHIGAN

MAINE

WISCONSIN

VT. N.H.

NEW YORK

MASS.
CONN. R.I.

NEVADA TERRITORY

UTAH TERRITORY

NEBRASKA TERRITORY

IOWA

PENNSYLVANIA

N.J.

CALIFORNIA

COLORADO TERRITORY

KANSAS 1861

ILLINOIS

INDIANA

OHIO

MASON–DIXON LINE

MD.

DEL.

MISSOURI

VIRGINIA

KENTUCKY

PUBLIC LAND

INDIAN TERRITORY

TENNESSEE

NORTH CAROLINA

NEW MEXICO TERRITORY

ARKANSAS

SOUTH CAROLINA

MISSISSIPPI

ALABAMA

GEORGIA

TEXAS

LOUISIANA

FLORIDA

FREE STATES

SLAVE STATES

TERRITORIES OPEN TO SLAVERY BY DRED SCOTT DECISION 1857

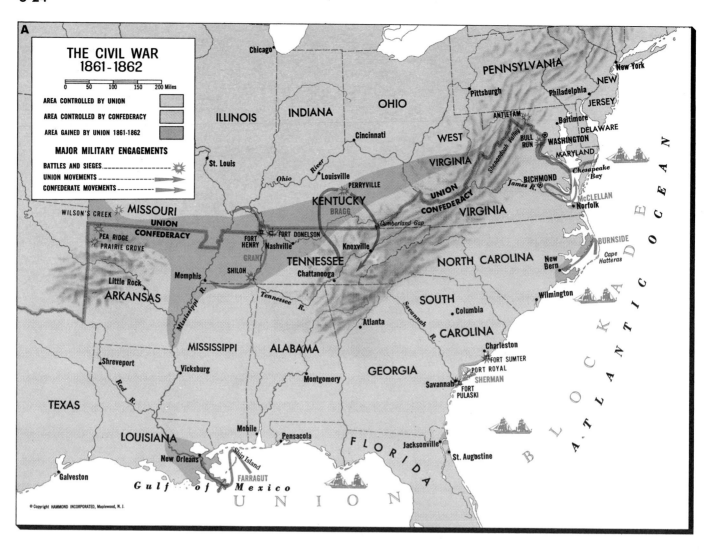

THE CIVIL WAR
1861-1862

0 50 100 150 200 Miles

AREA CONTROLLED BY UNION
AREA CONTROLLED BY CONFEDERACY
AREA GAINED BY UNION 1861-1862

MAJOR MILITARY ENGAGEMENTS

BATTLES AND SIEGES
UNION MOVEMENTS
CONFEDERATE MOVEMENTS

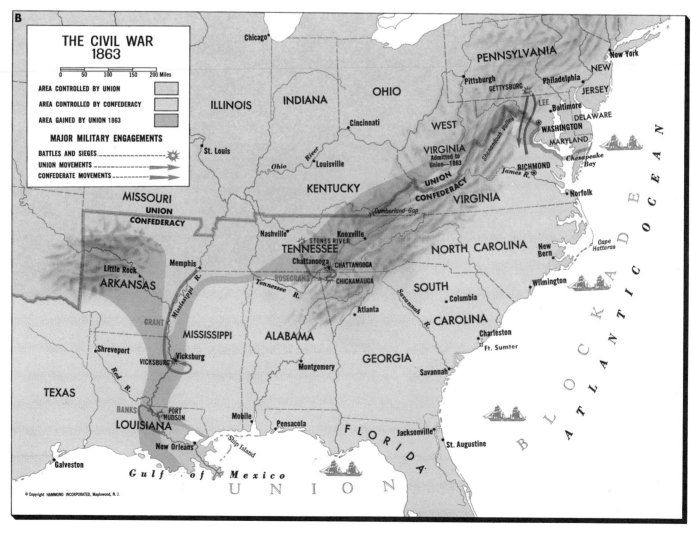

THE CIVIL WAR
1863

0 50 100 150 200 Miles

AREA CONTROLLED BY UNION
AREA CONTROLLED BY CONFEDERACY
AREA GAINED BY UNION 1863

MAJOR MILITARY ENGAGEMENTS

BATTLES AND SIEGES
UNION MOVEMENTS
CONFEDERATE MOVEMENTS

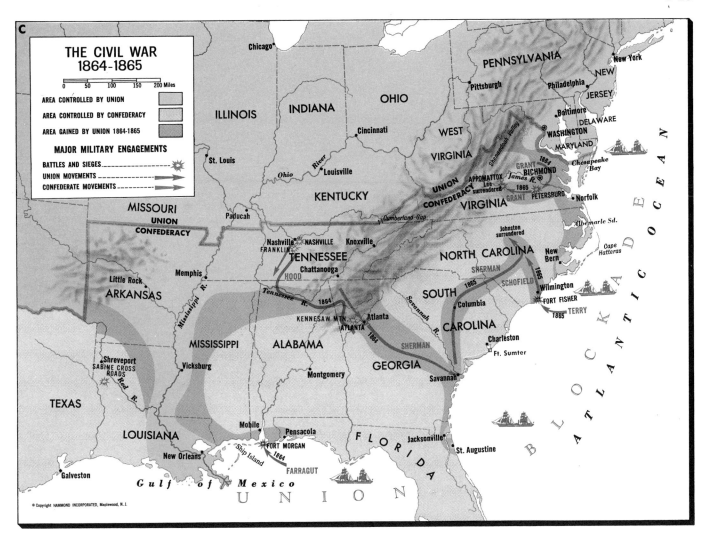

C

THE CIVIL WAR 1864-1865

0 50 100 150 200 Miles

AREA CONTROLLED BY UNION

AREA CONTROLLED BY CONFEDERACY

AREA GAINED BY UNION 1864-1865

MAJOR MILITARY ENGAGEMENTS

BATTLES AND SIEGES

UNION MOVEMENTS

CONFEDERATE MOVEMENTS

© Copyright HAMMOND INCORPORATED, Maplewood, N.J.

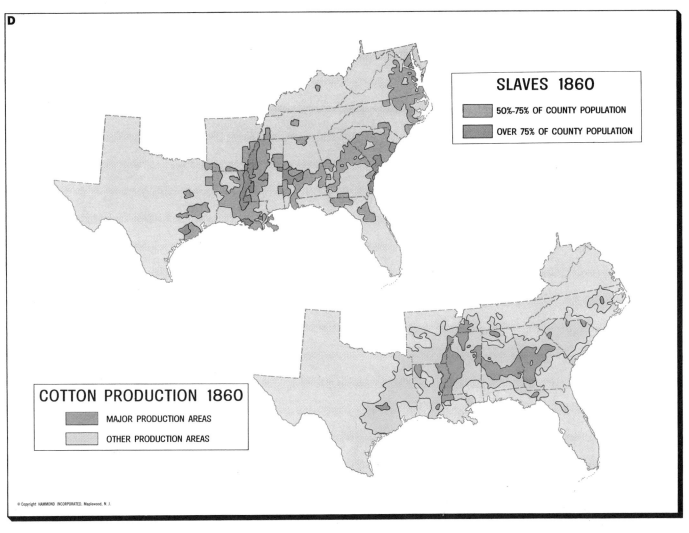

D

SLAVES 1860

50%-75% OF COUNTY POPULATION

OVER 75% OF COUNTY POPULATION

COTTON PRODUCTION 1860

MAJOR PRODUCTION AREAS

OTHER PRODUCTION AREAS

© Copyright HAMMOND INCORPORATED, Maplewood, N.J.

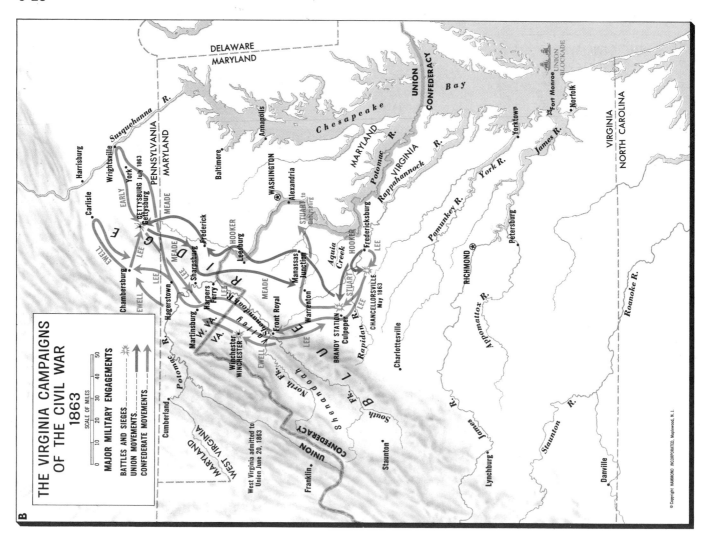

THE VIRGINIA CAMPAIGNS OF THE CIVIL WAR 1863

SCALE OF MILES

MAJOR MILITARY ENGAGEMENTS

BATTLES AND SIEGES
UNION MOVEMENTS
CONFEDERATE MOVEMENTS

West Virginia admitted to Union June 20, 1863

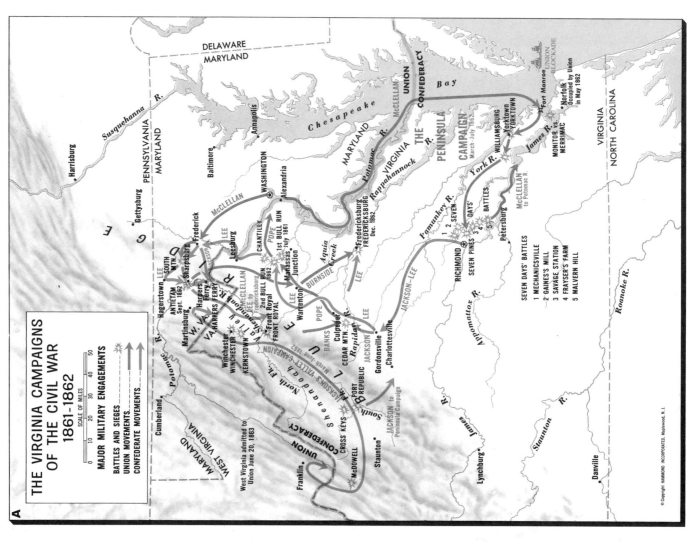

THE VIRGINIA CAMPAIGNS OF THE CIVIL WAR 1861-1862

SCALE OF MILES

MAJOR MILITARY ENGAGEMENTS

BATTLES AND SIEGES
UNION MOVEMENTS
CONFEDERATE MOVEMENTS

West Virginia admitted to Union June 20, 1863

SEVEN DAYS' BATTLES
1 MECHANICSVILLE
2 GAINES'S MILL
3 SAVAGE STATION
4 FRAYSER'S FARM
5 MALVERN HILL

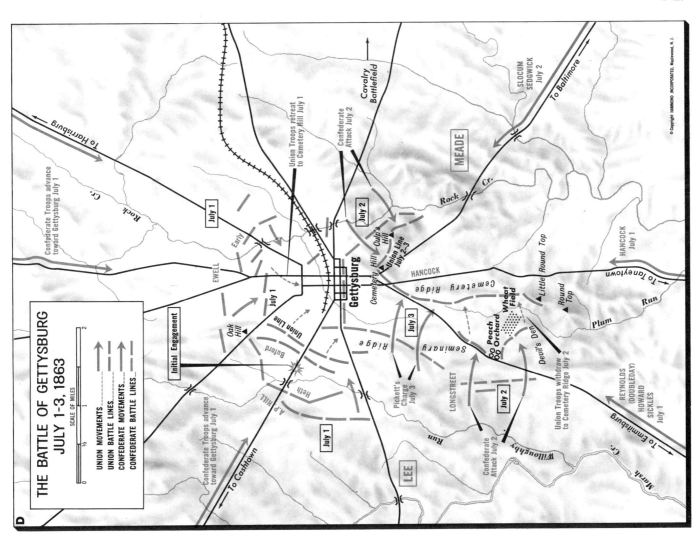

D

THE BATTLE OF GETTYSBURG
JULY 1-3, 1863

SCALE OF MILES

UNION MOVEMENTS
UNION BATTLE LINES
CONFEDERATE MOVEMENTS
CONFEDERATE BATTLE LINES

Confederate Troops advance toward Gettysburg July 1

To Harrisburg

To Cashtown

Rock Cr.

EWELL

Early

July 1

Union Troops retreat to Cemetery Hill July 1

Confederate Attack July 2

Cavalry Battlefield

Oak Hill

Initial Engagement

Buford

July 1

Heth

A.P. Hill

July 1

Union Line

Seminary Ridge

Gettysburg

Culp's Hill

Cemetery Hill

Union Line July 2-3

MEADE

Rock Cr.

HANCOCK

Cemetery Ridge

HANCOCK July 1

To Taneytown

LONGSTREET

Pickett's Charge July 3

July 3

July 2

Peach Orchard

Wheat Field

Devil's Den

Little Round Top

Round Top

Plum Run

LEE

Confederate Attack July 2

Willoughby Run

Union Troops withdraw to Cemetery Ridge July 2

REYNOLDS (DOUBLEDAY) HOWARD SICKLES July 1

To Emmitsburg

Marsh Cr.

SLOCUM SEDGWICK July 2

To Baltimore

Confederate Troops advance toward Gettysburg July 1

© Copyright HAMMOND INCORPORATED, Maplewood, N.J.

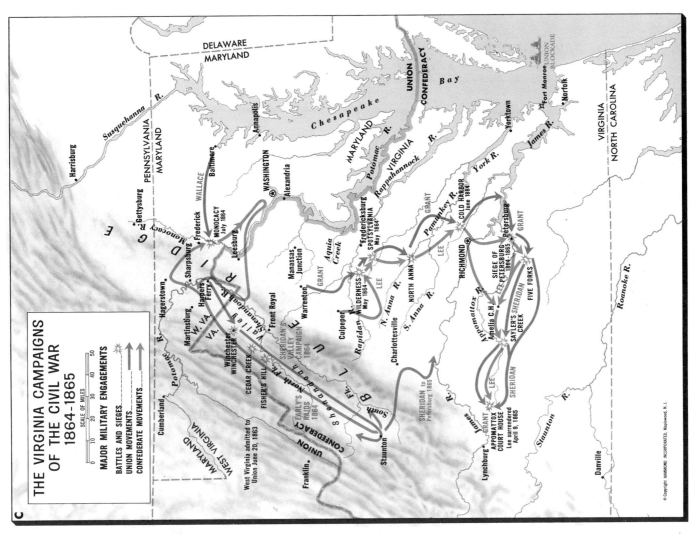

C

THE VIRGINIA CAMPAIGNS
OF THE CIVIL WAR
1864-1865

SCALE OF MILES
0 10 20 30 40 50

West Virginia admitted to Union June 20, 1863

MAJOR MILITARY ENGAGEMENTS

BATTLES AND SIEGES
UNION MOVEMENTS
CONFEDERATE MOVEMENTS

DELAWARE
MARYLAND

Chesapeake Bay

UNION
CONFEDERACY

PENNSYLVANIA
MARYLAND

Harrisburg

Susquehanna R.

Gettysburg

Cumberland

Potomac R.

Hagerstown

Martinsburg

Sharpsburg

Harper's Ferry

W. VA.
VA.

Winchester

WINCHESTER

CEDAR CREEK

FISHER'S HILL

EARLY'S RAIDS

North Fk.

South Fk.

Shenandoah

SHERIDAN'S VALLEY CAMPAIGN 1864

Front Royal

Warrenton

Manassas Junction

Leesburg

Frederick

MONOCACY July 1864

WALLACE

Monocacy R.

Baltimore

Annapolis

MARYLAND
VIRGINIA

WASHINGTON

Alexandria

Aquia Creek

GRANT

Fredericksburg

SPOTSYLVANIA May 1864

Rappahannock R.

Potomac R.

Culpeper

Rapidan R.

WILDERNESS May 1864

LEE

N. Anna R.

NORTH ANNA

Charlottesville

S. Anna R.

GRANT

Pamunkey R.

COLD HARBOR June 1864

LEE

RICHMOND

Appomattox R.

Amelia C.H.

SIEGE OF PETERSBURG 1864-1865

Petersburg

GRANT

FIVE FORKS

SHERIDAN

SAYLER'S CREEK

York R.

James R.

Yorktown

Fort Monroe

Norfolk

VIRGINIA
NORTH CAROLINA

Roanoke R.

SHERIDAN to Petersburg 1865

Staunton

James R.

Staunton R.

Lynchburg

APPOMATTOX COURT HOUSE
Lee surrendered April 9, 1865

GRANT

LEE

SHERIDAN

Danville

Franklin

WEST VIRGINIA

MARYLAND

UNION
CONFEDERACY

© Copyright HAMMOND INCORPORATED, Maplewood, N.J.

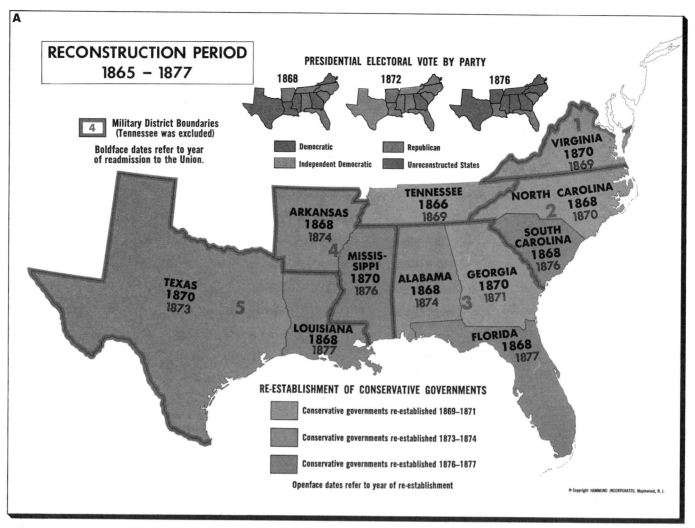

A

RECONSTRUCTION PERIOD 1865 – 1877

PRESIDENTIAL ELECTORAL VOTE BY PARTY

1868   1872   1876

- Democratic
- Independent Democratic
- Republican
- Unreconstructed States

4 Military District Boundaries (Tennessee was excluded)

Boldface dates refer to year of readmission to the Union.

VIRGINIA **1870** 1869

TENNESSEE **1866** 1869

NORTH CAROLINA **1868** 1870

ARKANSAS **1868** 1874

MISSIS-SIPPI **1870** 1876

SOUTH CAROLINA **1868** 1876

TEXAS **1870** 1873

ALABAMA **1868** 1874

GEORGIA **1870** 1871

LOUISIANA **1868** 1877

FLORIDA **1868** 1877

4   **5**   **3**

RE-ESTABLISHMENT OF CONSERVATIVE GOVERNMENTS

- Conservative governments re-established 1869–1871
- Conservative governments re-established 1873–1874
- Conservative governments re-established 1876–1877

Openface dates refer to year of re-establishment

© Copyright HAMMOND INCORPORATED, Maplewood, N. J.

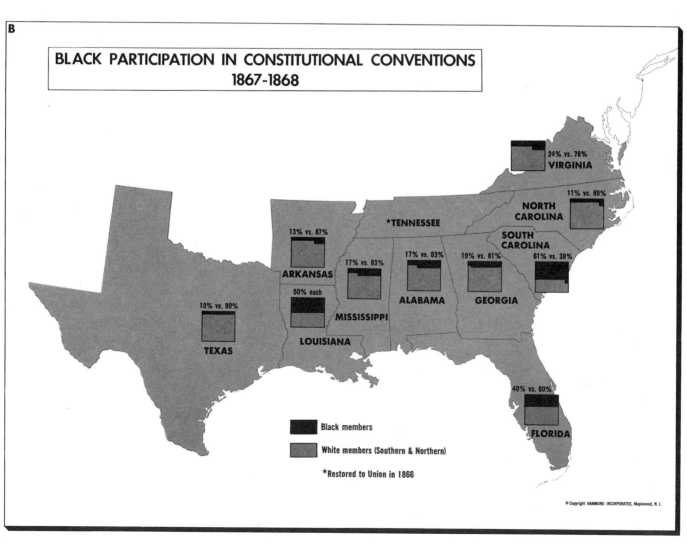

B

BLACK PARTICIPATION IN CONSTITUTIONAL CONVENTIONS 1867-1868

24% vs. 76% VIRGINIA

11% vs. 89% NORTH CAROLINA

*TENNESSEE

SOUTH CAROLINA

13% vs. 87% ARKANSAS

17% vs. 83%

17% vs. 83% ALABAMA

19% vs. 81% GEORGIA

61% vs. 39%

50% each MISSISSIPPI

10% vs. 90% TEXAS

LOUISIANA

40% vs. 60% FLORIDA

- Black members
- White members (Southern & Northern)

*Restored to Union in 1866

© Copyright HAMMOND INCORPORATED, Maplewood, N. J.

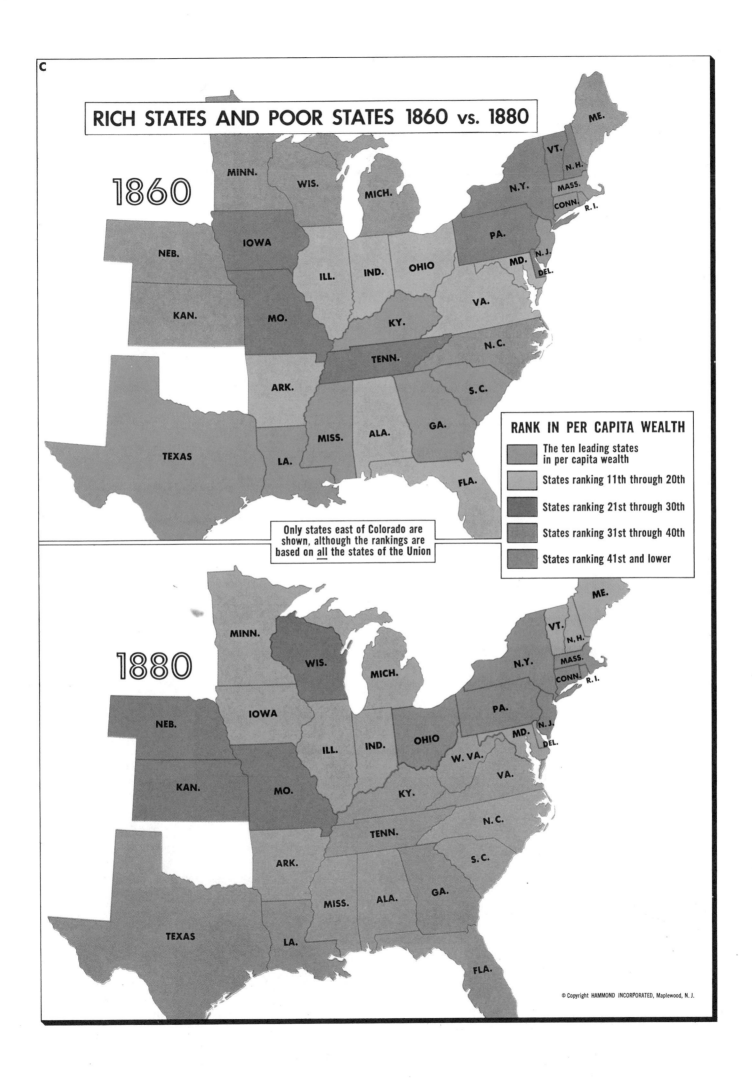

RICH STATES AND POOR STATES 1860 vs. 1880

1860

1880

Only states east of Colorado are shown, although the rankings are based on all the states of the Union

RANK IN PER CAPITA WEALTH

The ten leading states in per capita wealth

States ranking 11th through 20th

States ranking 21st through 30th

States ranking 31st through 40th

States ranking 41st and lower

© Copyright HAMMOND INCORPORATED, Maplewood, N. J.

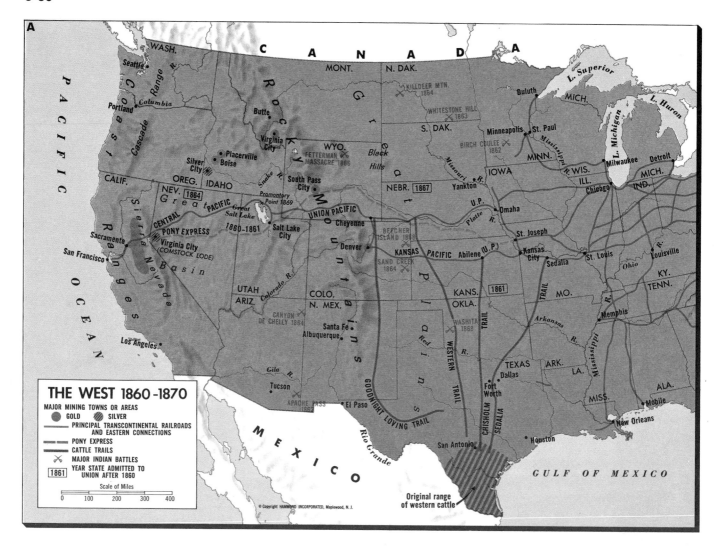

A

THE WEST 1860-1870

MAJOR MINING TOWNS OR AREAS
- ● GOLD
- ▨ SILVER
- ── PRINCIPAL TRANSCONTINENTAL RAILROADS AND EASTERN CONNECTIONS
- ┅ PONY EXPRESS
- ── CATTLE TRAILS
- ✕ MAJOR INDIAN BATTLES
- 1861 YEAR STATE ADMITTED TO UNION AFTER 1860

Scale of Miles
0   100   200   300   400

© Copyright HAMMOND INCORPORATED, Maplewood, N. J.

Original range of western cattle

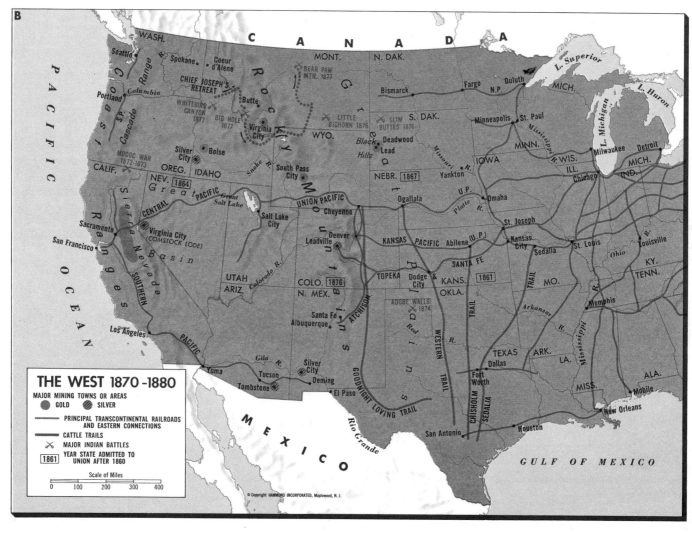

B

THE WEST 1870-1880

MAJOR MINING TOWNS OR AREAS
- ● GOLD
- ▨ SILVER
- ── PRINCIPAL TRANSCONTINENTAL RAILROADS AND EASTERN CONNECTIONS
- ── CATTLE TRAILS
- ✕ MAJOR INDIAN BATTLES
- 1861 YEAR STATE ADMITTED TO UNION AFTER 1860

Scale of Miles
0   100   200   300   400

© Copyright HAMMOND INCORPORATED, Maplewood, N. J.

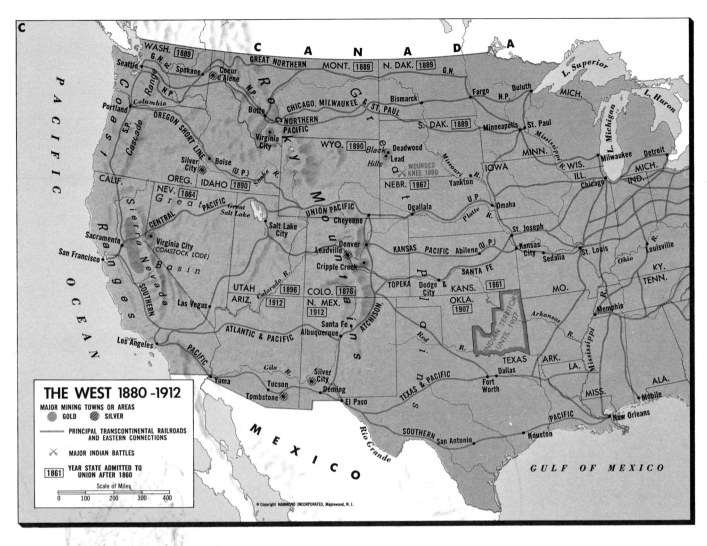

THE WEST 1880-1912

MAJOR MINING TOWNS OR AREAS
● GOLD ◿ SILVER

—— PRINCIPAL TRANSCONTINENTAL RAILROADS
AND EASTERN CONNECTIONS

✕ MAJOR INDIAN BATTLES

1861 YEAR STATE ADMITTED TO
UNION AFTER 1860

Scale of Miles
0 100 200 300 400

© Copyright HAMMOND INCORPORATED, Maplewood, N. J.

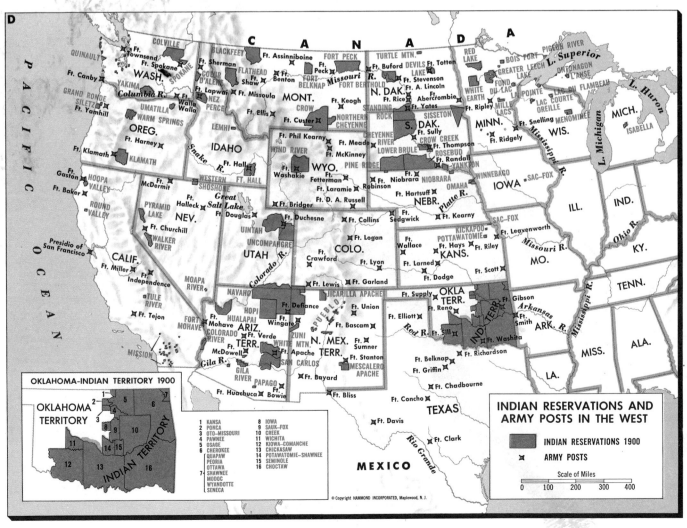

OKLAHOMA-INDIAN TERRITORY 1900

OKLAHOMA
TERRITORY

INDIAN TERRITORY

1 KANSA
2 PONCA
3 OTO-MISSOURI
4 PAWNEE
5 OSAGE
6 CHEROKEE
QUAPAW
PEORIA
OTTAWA
7 SHAWNEE
MODOC
WYANDOTTE
SENECA
8 IOWA
9 SAUK-FOX
10 CREEK
11 WICHITA
12 KIOWA-COMANCHE
13 CHICKASAW
14 POTAWATOMIE-SHAWNEE
15 SEMINOLE
16 CHOCTAW

INDIAN RESERVATIONS AND ARMY POSTS IN THE WEST

▬ INDIAN RESERVATIONS 1900
✕ ARMY POSTS

Scale of Miles
0 100 200 300 400

© Copyright HAMMOND INCORPORATED, Maplewood, N. J.

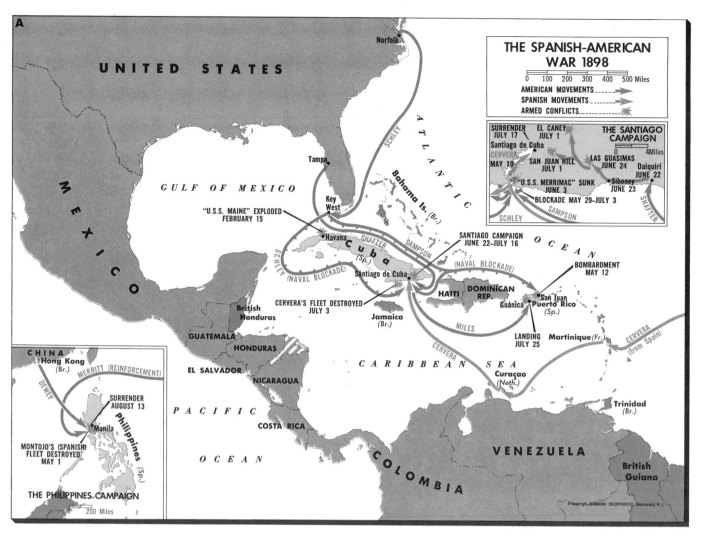

A

UNITED STATES

MEXICO

GULF OF MEXICO

Norfolk

Tampa

SCHLEY

ATLANTIC OCEAN

Bahama Is. (Br.)

THE SPANISH-AMERICAN WAR 1898

0 100 200 300 400 500 Miles

AMERICAN MOVEMENTS
SPANISH MOVEMENTS
ARMED CONFLICTS

THE SANTIAGO CAMPAIGN

SURRENDER JULY 17 — EL CANEY JULY 1
Santiago de Cuba
CERVERA MAY 19 — SAN JUAN HILL JULY 1 — LAS GUASIMAS JUNE 24
"U.S.S. MERRIMAC" SUNK JUNE 3
BLOCKADE MAY 29–JULY 3
SCHLEY   SAMPSON   SHAFTER
Daiquirí JUNE 22
Siboney JUNE 23

0   4 Miles

Key West

"U.S.S. MAINE" EXPLODED FEBRUARY 15

Havana Cuba (Sp.) SHAFTER
SCHLEY (NAVAL BLOCKADE)
SANTIAGO CAMPAIGN JUNE 22–JULY 16
(NAVAL BLOCKADE)

Santiago de Cuba
SAMPSON

CERVERA'S FLEET DESTROYED JULY 3

Jamaica (Br.)

HAITI   DOMINICAN REP.

BOMBARDMENT MAY 12

Guánica   San Juan
Puerto Rico (Sp.)

LANDING JULY 25   Martinique (Fr.)

MILES   CERVERA (from Spain)

CARIBBEAN SEA

British Honduras

GUATEMALA

HONDURAS

EL SALVADOR

NICARAGUA

COSTA RICA

CHINA
Hong Kong (Br.)
MERRITT (REINFORCEMENT)
DEWEY
SURRENDER AUGUST 13
Manila
MONTOJO'S (SPANISH) FLEET DESTROYED MAY 1
Philippines (Sp.)
THE PHILIPPINES CAMPAIGN
0   200 Miles

PACIFIC OCEAN

Curaçao (Neth.)

Trinidad (Br.)

VENEZUELA

COLOMBIA

British Guiana

© Copyright HAMMOND INCORPORATED, Maplewood, N.J.

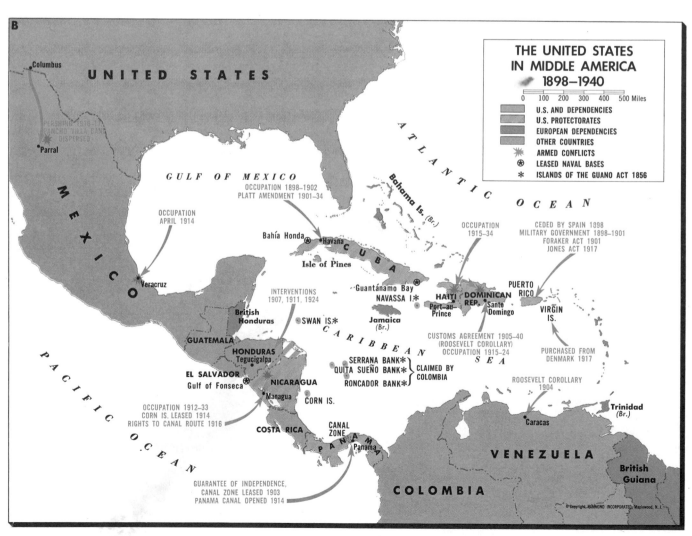

B

Columbus

UNITED STATES

PERSHING 1916–17
PANCHO VILLA BAND DISPERSED

Parral

MEXICO

GULF OF MEXICO

OCCUPATION 1898–1902
PLATT AMENDMENT 1901–34

OCCUPATION APRIL 1914

Bahama Is. (Br.)

ATLANTIC OCEAN

THE UNITED STATES IN MIDDLE AMERICA 1898–1940

0 100 200 300 400 500 Miles

U.S. AND DEPENDENCIES
U.S. PROTECTORATES
EUROPEAN DEPENDENCIES
OTHER COUNTRIES
ARMED CONFLICTS
LEASED NAVAL BASES
ISLANDS OF THE GUANO ACT 1856

Bahía Honda   Havana

Veracruz

Isle of Pines   CUBA

OCCUPATION 1915–34

CEDED BY SPAIN 1898
MILITARY GOVERNMENT 1898–1901
FORAKER ACT 1901
JONES ACT 1917

INTERVENTIONS 1907, 1911, 1924

Guantánamo Bay   NAVASSA I.*

PUERTO RICO

British Honduras

GUATEMALA

HONDURAS
Tegucigalpa

EL SALVADOR
Gulf of Fonseca

NICARAGUA
Managua

SWAN IS.*

Jamaica (Br.)

CARIBBEAN

HAITI   DOMINICAN REP.
Port-au-Prince   Santo Domingo

VIRGIN IS.

PURCHASED FROM DENMARK 1917

SEA

CUSTOMS AGREEMENT 1905–40 (ROOSEVELT COROLLARY)
OCCUPATION 1915–24

SERRANA BANK*
QUITA SUEÑO BANK*   CLAIMED BY COLOMBIA
RONCADOR BANK*

ROOSEVELT COROLLARY 1904

CORN IS.

OCCUPATION 1912–33
CORN IS. LEASED 1914
RIGHTS TO CANAL ROUTE 1916

COSTA RICA

CANAL ZONE
PANAMA   Panama

PACIFIC OCEAN

GUARANTEE OF INDEPENDENCE, CANAL ZONE LEASED 1903
PANAMA CANAL OPENED 1914

Trinidad (Br.)

Caracas

VENEZUELA

COLOMBIA

British Guiana

© Copyright HAMMOND INCORPORATED, Maplewood, N.J.

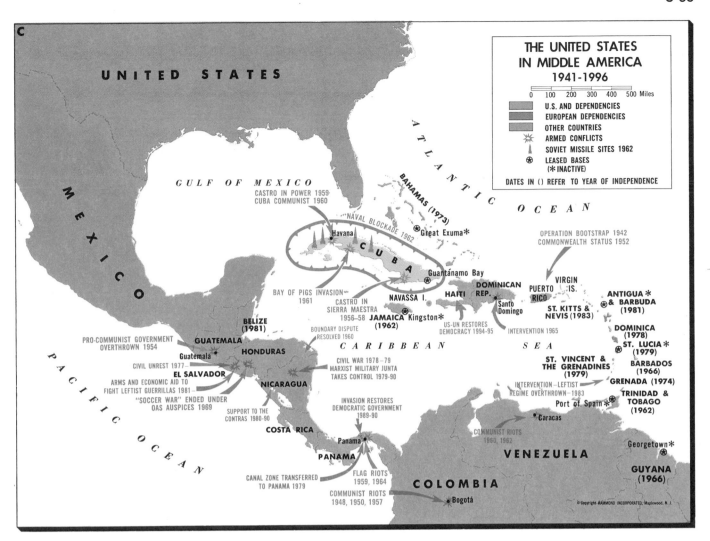

C

THE UNITED STATES IN MIDDLE AMERICA
1941-1996

0 100 200 300 400 500 Miles

- U.S. AND DEPENDENCIES
- EUROPEAN DEPENDENCIES
- OTHER COUNTRIES
- ✳ ARMED CONFLICTS
- ▲ SOVIET MISSILE SITES 1962
- ⊛ LEASED BASES (✳ INACTIVE)

DATES IN ( ) REFER TO YEAR OF INDEPENDENCE

UNITED STATES

GULF OF MEXICO

MEXICO

PACIFIC OCEAN

ATLANTIC OCEAN

BAHAMAS (1973)

CASTRO IN POWER 1959
CUBA COMMUNIST 1960

NAVAL BLOCKADE 1962

Havana

⊛ Great Exuma ✳

CUBA

Guantánamo Bay

BAY OF PIGS INVASION 1961

CASTRO IN SIERRA MAESTRA 1956–58

NAVASSA I.

HAITI

JAMAICA Kingston ✳
(1962)

BOUNDARY DISPUTE RESOLVED 1960

DOMINICAN REP.
Santo Domingo

US-UN RESTORES DEMOCRACY 1994-95

INTERVENTION 1965

OPERATION BOOTSTRAP 1942
COMMONWEALTH STATUS 1952

VIRGIN IS.
PUERTO RICO

ANTIGUA ✳ & BARBUDA (1981)

ST. KITTS & NEVIS (1983)

DOMINICA (1978)

ST. LUCIA ✳ (1979)

BELIZE (1981)

PRO-COMMUNIST GOVERNMENT OVERTHROWN 1954

GUATEMALA

HONDURAS

Guatemala

CIVIL UNREST 1977–

EL SALVADOR

ARMS AND ECONOMIC AID TO FIGHT LEFTIST GUERRILLAS 1981–

"SOCCER WAR" ENDED UNDER OAS AUSPICES 1969

NICARAGUA

CIVIL WAR 1978–79
MARXIST MILITARY JUNTA TAKES CONTROL 1979-90

SUPPORT TO THE CONTRAS 1980-90

COSTA RICA

INVASION RESTORES DEMOCRATIC GOVERNMENT 1989-90

PANAMA

Panama

CANAL ZONE TRANSFERRED TO PANAMA 1979

FLAG RIOTS 1959, 1964

COMMUNIST RIOTS 1948, 1950, 1957

Bogotá

COLOMBIA

CARIBBEAN SEA

ST. VINCENT & THE GRENADINES (1979)

BARBADOS (1966)

GRENADA (1974)

INTERVENTION–LEFTIST REGIME OVERTHROWN–1983

Port of Spain ⊛ ✳

TRINIDAD & TOBAGO (1962)

Caracas

COMMUNIST RIOTS 1960, 1962

VENEZUELA

Georgetown ✳ ⊛

GUYANA (1966)

© Copyright HAMMOND INCORPORATED, Maplewood, N.J.

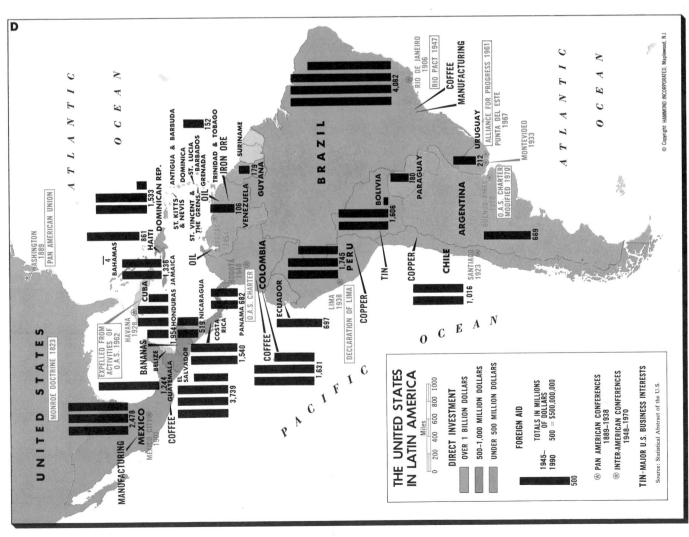

D

© Copyright HAMMOND INCORPORATED, Maplewood, N.J.

THE UNITED STATES IN LATIN AMERICA

0 200 400 600 800 1000 Miles

DIRECT INVESTMENT
- OVER 1 BILLION DOLLARS
- 500–1,000 MILLION DOLLARS
- UNDER 500 MILLION DOLLARS

FOREIGN AID
TOTALS IN MILLIONS OF DOLLARS
500 = $500,000,000

1945– 1990

500

⊛ PAN AMERICAN CONFERENCES 1889–1938
⊛ INTER-AMERICAN CONFERENCES 1948-1970

TIN–MAJOR U.S. BUSINESS INTERESTS

Source: Statistical Abstract of the U.S.

ATLANTIC OCEAN

PACIFIC OCEAN

UNITED STATES

MONROE DOCTRINE 1823

MANUFACTURING

WASHINGTON 1889
PAN AMERICAN UNION

Mexico City ⊛ 1901

MEXICO 2,478

COFFEE

EXPELLED FROM ACTIVITIES OF O.A.S. 1962

HAVANA 1928 ⊛

CUBA

BANANAS

BELIZE

1,244 GUATEMALA

EL SALVADOR

DOMINICAN REP. 1,533

HAITI 861

BAHAMAS 4

1,336 JAMAICA

1,954 HONDURAS

519 NICARAGUA

1,540 COSTA RICA

Panama 682

O.A.S. CHARTER

ANTIGUA & BARBUDA 152
IRON ORE

ST. KITTS & NEVIS
DOMINICA
ST. LUCIA
ST. VINCENT & THE GRENS.
BARBADOS
GRENADA
TRINIDAD & TOBAGO 179
OIL

SURINAME

CARACAS 1954

VENEZUELA 106

GUYANA

COLOMBIA

BOGOTA 1948

OIL

ECUADOR

697

COFFEE

COPPER

1,745 PERU

LIMA 1938
DECLARATION OF LIMA

1,631

3,739

BRAZIL

RIO DE JANEIRO 1906
RIO PACT 1947

COFFEE
MANUFACTURING

4,082

ALLIANCE FOR PROGRESS 1961
PUNTA DEL ESTE 1967

URUGUAY 212

MONTEVIDEO 1933

O.A.S. CHARTER MODIFIED 1970

BUENOS AIRES

ARGENTINA 669

TIN

1,606 BOLIVIA

PARAGUAY 180

COPPER

CHILE 1,016

SANTIAGO 1923

ATLANTIC OCEAN

PACIFIC OCEAN

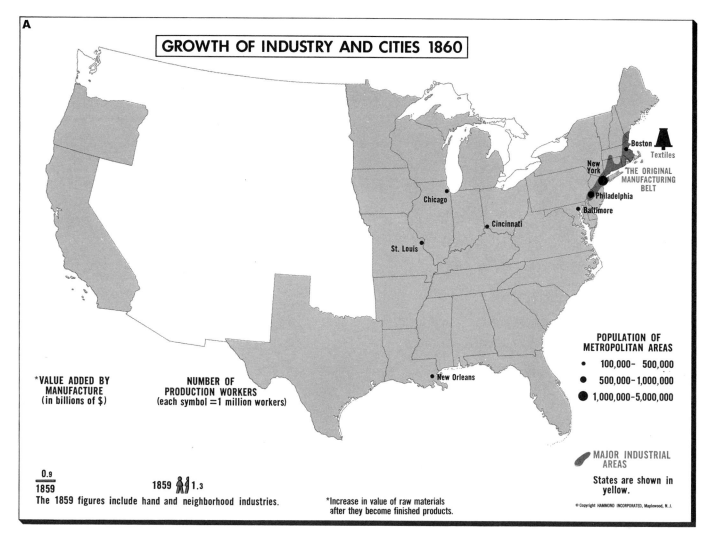

A

GROWTH OF INDUSTRY AND CITIES 1860

Boston

Textiles

New
York

THE ORIGINAL
MANUFACTURING
BELT

Chicago

Philadelphia

Baltimore

Cincinnati

St. Louis

New Orleans

**POPULATION OF
METROPOLITAN AREAS**

• 100,000- 500,000

● 500,000-1,000,000

● 1,000,000-5,000,000

*VALUE ADDED BY
MANUFACTURE
(in billions of $)

NUMBER OF
PRODUCTION WORKERS
(each symbol =1 million workers)

0.9
1859

1859 1.3

The 1859 figures include hand and neighborhood industries.

*Increase in value of raw materials
after they become finished products.

**MAJOR INDUSTRIAL
AREAS**

States are shown in
yellow.

© Copyright HAMMOND INCORPORATED, Maplewood, N. J.

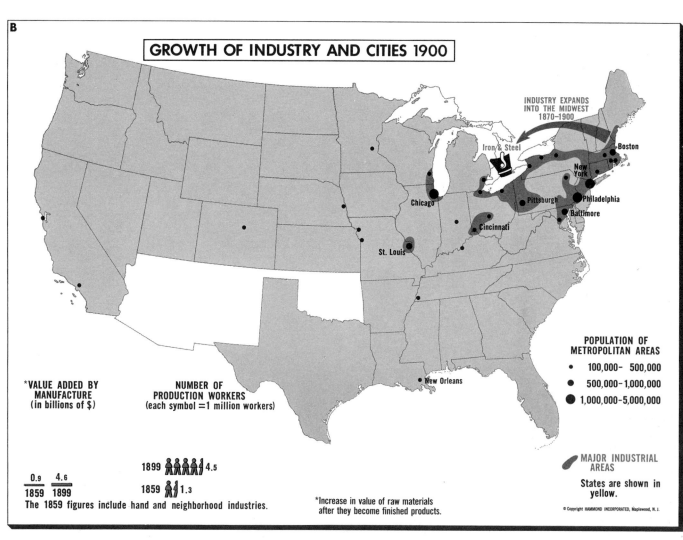

B

GROWTH OF INDUSTRY AND CITIES 1900

INDUSTRY EXPANDS
INTO THE MIDWEST
1870–1900

Iron & Steel

Boston

New
York

Chicago

Pittsburgh

Philadelphia

Baltimore

Cincinnati

St. Louis

New Orleans

**POPULATION OF
METROPOLITAN AREAS**

• 100,000- 500,000

● 500,000-1,000,000

● 1,000,000-5,000,000

*VALUE ADDED BY
MANUFACTURE
(in billions of $)

NUMBER OF
PRODUCTION WORKERS
(each symbol =1 million workers)

1899 4.5

0.9   4.6
1859   1899

1859 1.3

The 1859 figures include hand and neighborhood industries.

*Increase in value of raw materials
after they become finished products.

**MAJOR INDUSTRIAL
AREAS**

States are shown in
yellow.

© Copyright HAMMOND INCORPORATED, Maplewood, N. J.

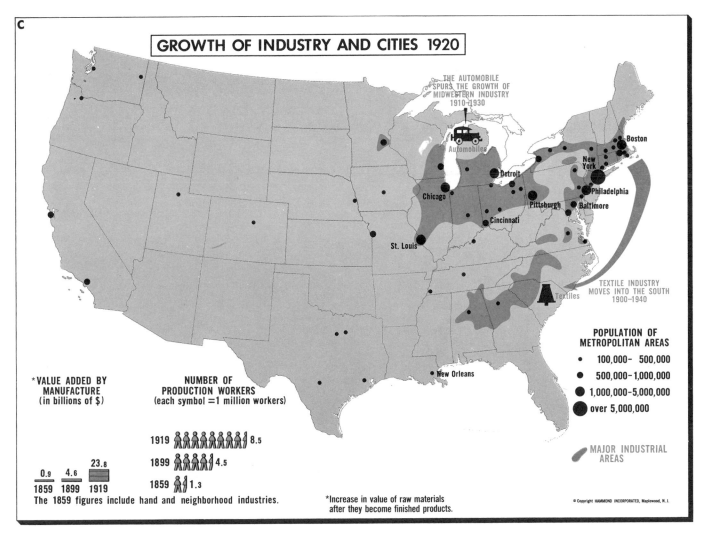

C

GROWTH OF INDUSTRY AND CITIES 1920

THE AUTOMOBILE
SPURS THE GROWTH OF
MIDWESTERN INDUSTRY
1910-1930

Automobiles

TEXTILE INDUSTRY
MOVES INTO THE SOUTH
1900-1940

Textiles

Boston

New York

Detroit

Chicago

Philadelphia

Pittsburgh   Baltimore

Cincinnati

St. Louis

New Orleans

**POPULATION OF
METROPOLITAN AREAS**

· 100,000- 500,000

● 500,000-1,000,000

● 1,000,000-5,000,000

● over 5,000,000

*VALUE ADDED BY
MANUFACTURE
(in billions of $)

NUMBER OF
PRODUCTION WORKERS
(each symbol =1 million workers)

1919 8.5

1899 4.5

1859 1.3

0.9   4.6   23.8
1859 1899 1919

The 1859 figures include hand and neighborhood industries.

*Increase in value of raw materials
after they become finished products.

MAJOR INDUSTRIAL
AREAS

© Copyright HAMMOND INCORPORATED, Maplewood, N.J.

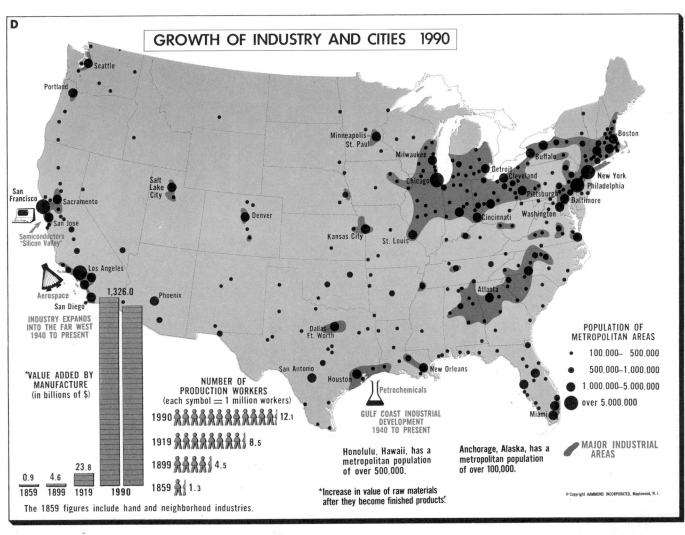

D

GROWTH OF INDUSTRY AND CITIES 1990

Seattle

Portland

Minneapolis-
St. Paul

Milwaukee

Boston

Buffalo

Detroit Cleveland

New York

San
Francisco

Sacramento

Salt
Lake
City

Denver

Chicago

Pittsburgh

Philadelphia

Baltimore

San Jose

Semiconductors
"Silicon Valley"

Kansas City

St. Louis

Cincinnati

Washington

Los Angeles

Aerospace

San Diego

Phoenix

Atlanta

1,326.0

INDUSTRY EXPANDS
INTO THE FAR WEST
1940 TO PRESENT

Dallas-
Ft. Worth

San Antonio

New Orleans

Houston

Petrochemicals

GULF COAST INDUSTRIAL
DEVELOPMENT
1940 TO PRESENT

Miami

**POPULATION OF
METROPOLITAN AREAS**

· 100,000- 500,000

· 500,000-1,000,000

● 1,000,000-5,000,000

● over 5,000,000

*VALUE ADDED BY
MANUFACTURE
(in billions of $)

NUMBER OF
PRODUCTION WORKERS
(each symbol = 1 million workers)

1990 12.1

1919 8.5

1899 4.5

1859 1.3

0.9   4.6   23.8   1990
1859 1899 1919

The 1859 figures include hand and neighborhood industries.

Honolulu, Hawaii, has a
metropolitan population
of over 500,000.

Anchorage, Alaska, has a
metropolitan population
of over 100,000.

*Increase in value of raw materials
after they become finished products.

MAJOR INDUSTRIAL
AREAS

© Copyright HAMMOND INCORPORATED, Maplewood, N.J.

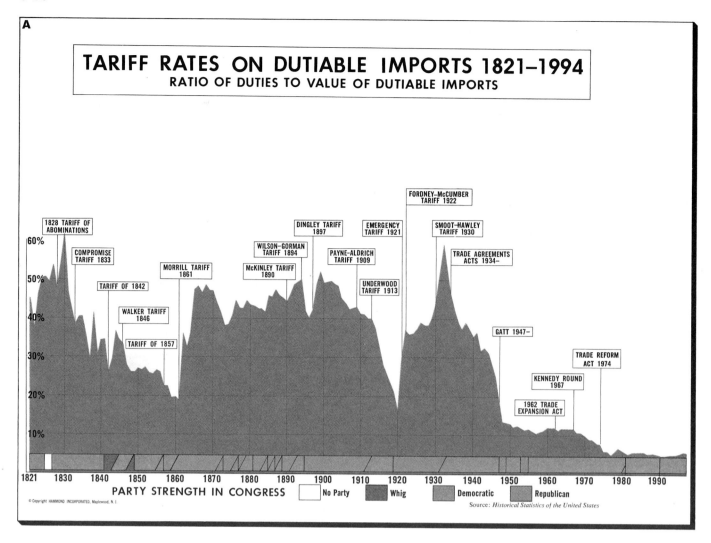

TARIFF RATES ON DUTIABLE IMPORTS 1821–1994
RATIO OF DUTIES TO VALUE OF DUTIABLE IMPORTS

1828 TARIFF OF ABOMINATIONS

COMPROMISE TARIFF 1833

TARIFF OF 1842

WALKER TARIFF 1846

TARIFF OF 1857

MORRILL TARIFF 1861

McKINLEY TARIFF 1890

WILSON–GORMAN TARIFF 1894

DINGLEY TARIFF 1897

PAYNE–ALDRICH TARIFF 1909

UNDERWOOD TARIFF 1913

EMERGENCY TARIFF 1921

FORDNEY–McCUMBER TARIFF 1922

SMOOT–HAWLEY TARIFF 1930

TRADE AGREEMENTS ACTS 1934–

GATT 1947–

1962 TRADE EXPANSION ACT

KENNEDY ROUND 1967

TRADE REFORM ACT 1974

60% 50% 40% 30% 20% 10%

1821 1830 1840 1850 1860 1870 1880 1890 1900 1910 1920 1930 1940 1950 1960 1970 1980 1990

PARTY STRENGTH IN CONGRESS   No Party   Whig   Democratic   Republican

© Copyright HAMMOND INCORPORATED, Maplewood, N.J.

Source: *Historical Statistics of the United States*

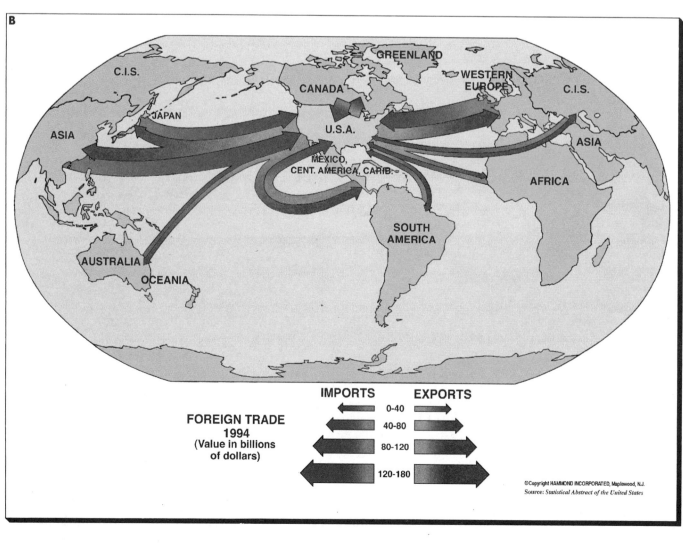

GREENLAND

C.I.S.

CANADA

WESTERN EUROPE

C.I.S.

JAPAN

ASIA

U.S.A.

ASIA

MEXICO, CENT. AMERICA, CARIB.

AFRICA

SOUTH AMERICA

AUSTRALIA

OCEANIA

IMPORTS   EXPORTS

FOREIGN TRADE 1994
(Value in billions of dollars)

0-40
40-80
80-120
120-180

©Copyright HAMMOND INCORPORATED, Maplewood, N.J.

Source: *Statistical Abstract of the United States*

C

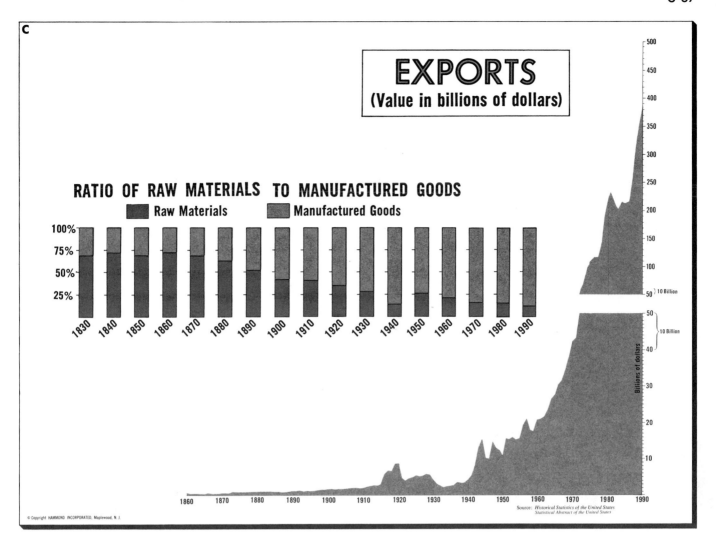

EXPORTS
(Value in billions of dollars)

RATIO OF RAW MATERIALS TO MANUFACTURED GOODS

■ Raw Materials ▨ Manufactured Goods

Source: *Historical Statistics of the United States*
Statistical Abstract of the United States

© Copyright HAMMOND INCORPORATED, Maplewood, N. J.

D

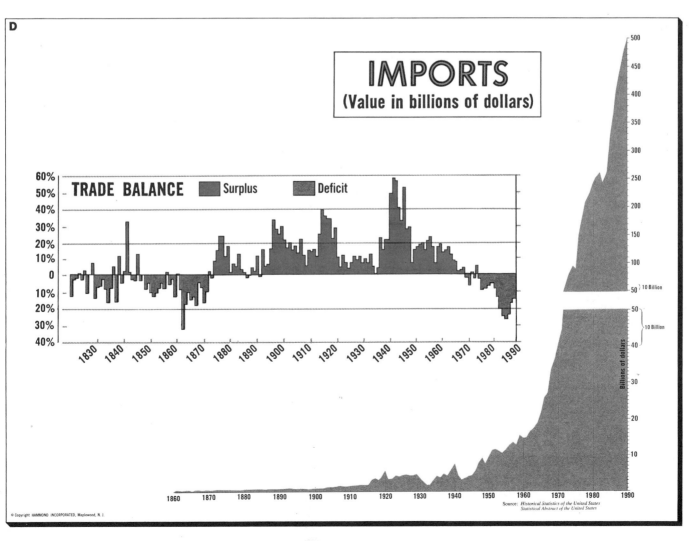

IMPORTS
(Value in billions of dollars)

TRADE BALANCE ▨ Surplus ▨ Deficit

Source: *Historical Statistics of the United States*
Statistical Abstract of the United States

© Copyright HAMMOND INCORPORATED, Maplewood, N. J.

A

SOURCES OF IMMIGRATION
1820–1990

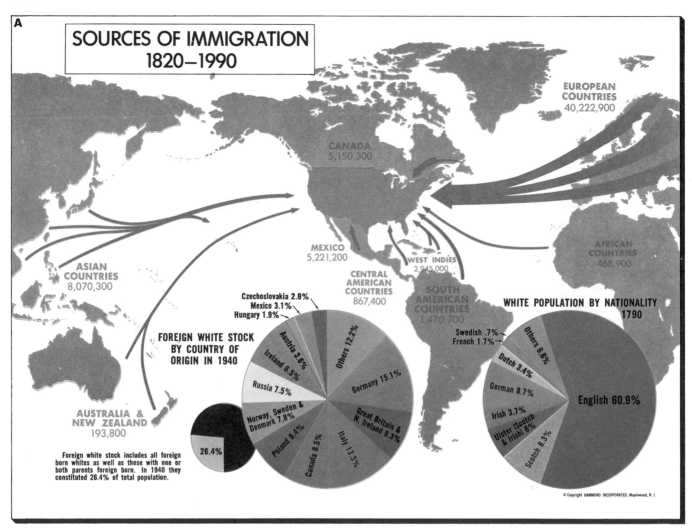

EUROPEAN COUNTRIES
40,222,900

CANADA
5,150,300

ASIAN COUNTRIES
8,070,300

AFRICAN COUNTRIES
468,900

MEXICO
5,221,200

WEST INDIES
2,945,000

CENTRAL AMERICAN COUNTRIES
867,400

SOUTH AMERICAN COUNTRIES
1,470,700

AUSTRALIA & NEW ZEALAND
193,800

FOREIGN WHITE STOCK BY COUNTRY OF ORIGIN IN 1940

Czechoslovakia 2.8%
Mexico 3.1%
Hungary 1.9%
Austria 3.6%
Ireland 6.5%
Russia 7.5%
Norway, Sweden & Denmark 7.8%
Poland 8.4%
Canada 8.5%
Italy 13.3%
Great Britain & N. Ireland 8.3%
Germany 15.1%
Others 12.2%

26.4%

Foreign white stock includes all foreign born whites as well as those with one or both parents foreign born. In 1940 they constituted 26.4% of total population.

WHITE POPULATION BY NATIONALITY 1790

Swedish .7%
French 1.7%
Others 6.6%
Dutch 3.4%
German 8.7%
Irish 3.7%
Ulster (Scotch & Irish) 6%
Scotch 8.3%
English 60.9%

© Copyright HAMMOND INCORPORATED, Maplewood, N.J.

B

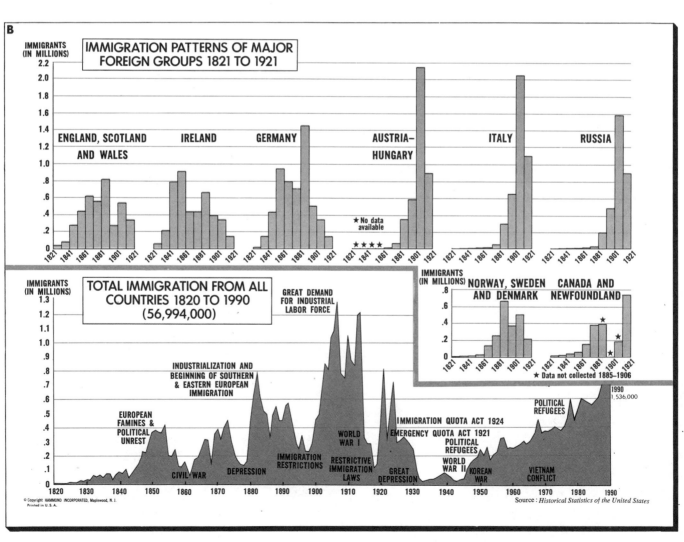

IMMIGRANTS (IN MILLIONS)

IMMIGRATION PATTERNS OF MAJOR FOREIGN GROUPS 1821 TO 1921

ENGLAND, SCOTLAND AND WALES

IRELAND

GERMANY

AUSTRIA–HUNGARY
★ No data available
★★★★

ITALY

RUSSIA

1821 1841 1861 1881 1901 1921

IMMIGRANTS (IN MILLIONS)

TOTAL IMMIGRATION FROM ALL COUNTRIES 1820 TO 1990
(56,994,000)

GREAT DEMAND FOR INDUSTRIAL LABOR FORCE

INDUSTRIALIZATION AND BEGINNING OF SOUTHERN & EASTERN EUROPEAN IMMIGRATION

EUROPEAN FAMINES & POLITICAL UNREST

CIVIL WAR

DEPRESSION

IMMIGRATION RESTRICTIONS

RESTRICTIVE IMMIGRATION LAWS

WORLD WAR I

IMMIGRATION QUOTA ACT 1924

EMERGENCY QUOTA ACT 1921
POLITICAL REFUGEES

GREAT DEPRESSION

WORLD WAR II

KOREAN WAR

VIETNAM CONFLICT

POLITICAL REFUGEES

1990
1,536,000

IMMIGRANTS (IN MILLIONS)

NORWAY, SWEDEN AND DENMARK

CANADA AND NEWFOUNDLAND

★ Data not collected 1885–1906

1821 1841 1861 1881 1901 1921

1820 1830 1840 1850 1860 1870 1880 1890 1900 1910 1920 1930 1940 1950 1960 1970 1980 1990

© Copyright HAMMOND INCORPORATED, Maplewood, N.J.
Printed in U.S.A.

Source: *Historical Statistics of the United States*

DISTRIBUTION OF FOREIGN BORN IN UNITED STATES
1910

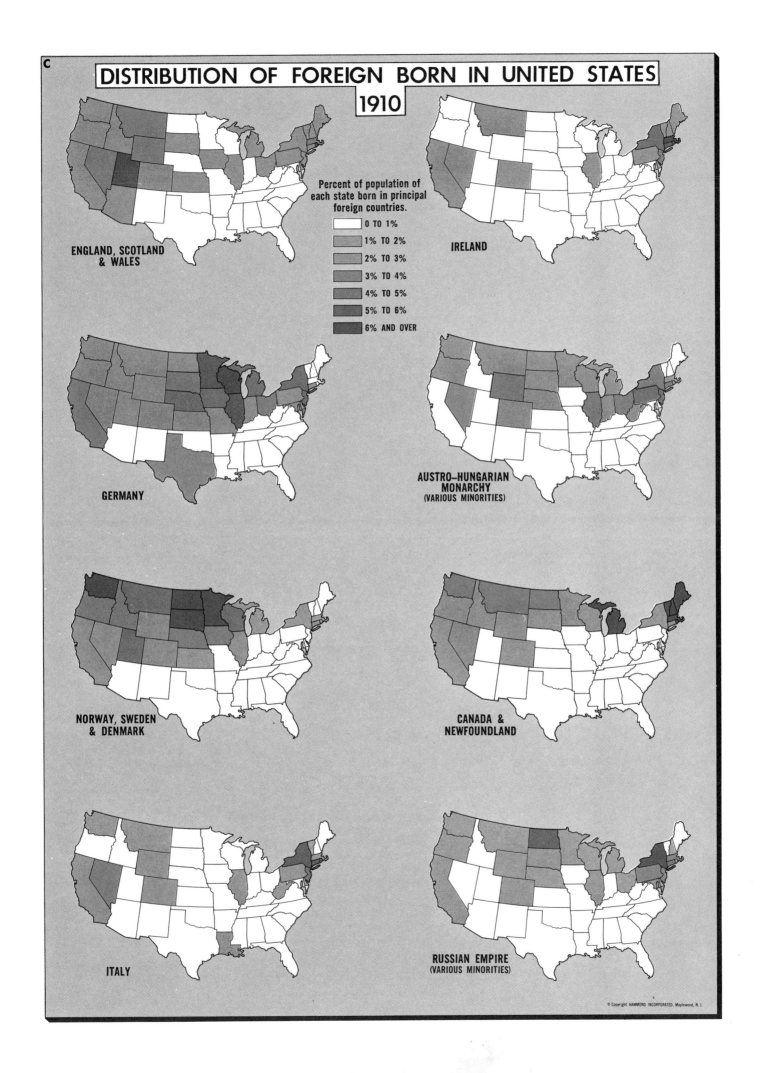

Percent of population of each state born in principal foreign countries.

- 0 TO 1%
- 1% TO 2%
- 2% TO 3%
- 3% TO 4%
- 4% TO 5%
- 5% TO 6%
- 6% AND OVER

ENGLAND, SCOTLAND & WALES

IRELAND

GERMANY

AUSTRO–HUNGARIAN MONARCHY
(VARIOUS MINORITIES)

NORWAY, SWEDEN & DENMARK

CANADA & NEWFOUNDLAND

ITALY

RUSSIAN EMPIRE
(VARIOUS MINORITIES)

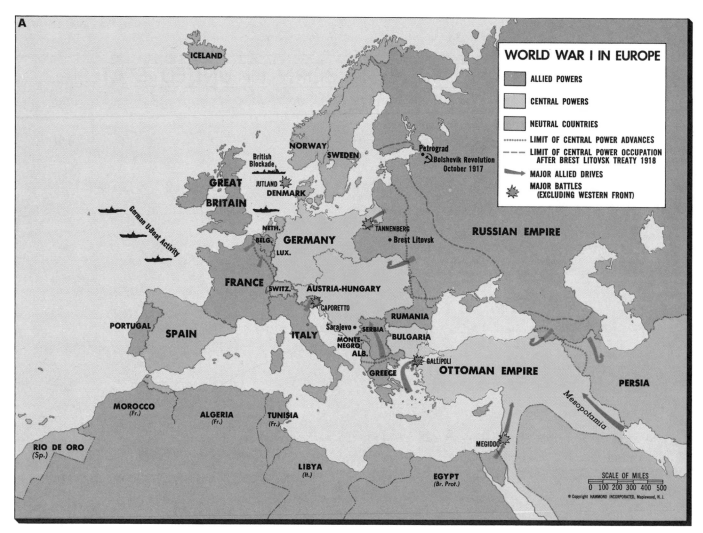

A

ICELAND

WORLD WAR I IN EUROPE

ALLIED POWERS

CENTRAL POWERS

NEUTRAL COUNTRIES

········ LIMIT OF CENTRAL POWER ADVANCES

— — — LIMIT OF CENTRAL POWER OCCUPATION
AFTER BREST LITOVSK TREATY 1918

➤ MAJOR ALLIED DRIVES

✷ MAJOR BATTLES
(EXCLUDING WESTERN FRONT)

NORWAY

British
Blockade

SWEDEN

Petrograd
Bolshevik Revolution
October 1917

GREAT
BRITAIN

JUTLAND
DENMARK

German U-Boat Activity

NETH.

BELG.

GERMANY

LUX.

Tannenberg

• Brest Litovsk

RUSSIAN EMPIRE

FRANCE

SWITZ.

AUSTRIA-HUNGARY

CAPORETTO

PORTUGAL

SPAIN

ITALY

Sarajevo

SERBIA

MONTE-
NEGRO
ALB.

RUMANIA

BULGARIA

GREECE

GALLIPOLI

OTTOMAN EMPIRE

PERSIA

MOROCCO
(Fr.)

ALGERIA
(Fr.)

TUNISIA
(Fr.)

MEGIDDO

Mesopotamia

RIO DE ORO
(Sp.)

LIBYA
(It.)

EGYPT
(Br. Prot.)

SCALE OF MILES
0 100 200 300 400 500

© Copyright HAMMOND INCORPORATED, Maplewood, N.J.

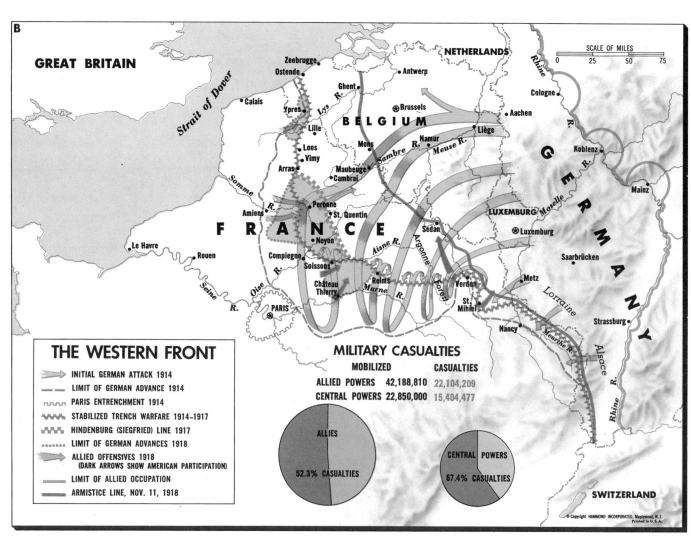

B

GREAT BRITAIN

NETHERLANDS

SCALE OF MILES
0   25   50   75

Zeebrugge
Ostende

• Antwerp

Rhine R.

Calais

Strait of Dover

Ghent •

⊕ Brussels

Cologne •

Ypres

Lys R.

BELGIUM

• Aachen

Lille

Mons •

Namur

Liège

Koblenz •

Loos

Vimy

Maubeuge

Sambre R.

Meuse R.

Rhine R.

Arras

Cambrai

G

Mainz •

Somme R.

Péronne

St. Quentin

LUXEMBURG

Moselle R.

E

Amiens

F R A N C E

Sedan

⊕ Luxemburg

R

Le Havre •

Noyon

Aisne R.

Argonne

Saarbrücken •

M

Rouen •

Compiegne

Soissons

Forest

Verdun

Metz •

A

Oise R.

Château
Thierry

Reims

Marne R.

St.
Mihiel

Lorraine

N

Seine R.

⊕ PARIS

Nancy •

Meurthe R.

Strassburg •

Y

Alsace

Rhine R.

THE WESTERN FRONT

➤ INITIAL GERMAN ATTACK 1914

— — — LIMIT OF GERMAN ADVANCE 1914

ᴖᴖᴖ PARIS ENTRENCHMENT 1914

ᐷᐷᐷ STABILIZED TRENCH WARFARE 1914–1917

▨▨▨ HINDENBURG (SIEGFRIED) LINE 1917

········ LIMIT OF GERMAN ADVANCES 1918

➤ ALLIED OFFENSIVES 1918
(DARK ARROWS SHOW AMERICAN PARTICIPATION)

——— LIMIT OF ALLIED OCCUPATION

——— ARMISTICE LINE, NOV. 11, 1918

MILITARY CASUALTIES

	MOBILIZED	CASUALTIES
ALLIED POWERS	42,188,810	22,104,209
CENTRAL POWERS	22,850,000	15,404,477

ALLIES

52.3% CASUALTIES

CENTRAL POWERS

67.4% CASUALTIES

SWITZERLAND

© Copyright HAMMOND INCORPORATED, Maplewood, N.J.
Printed in U.S.A.

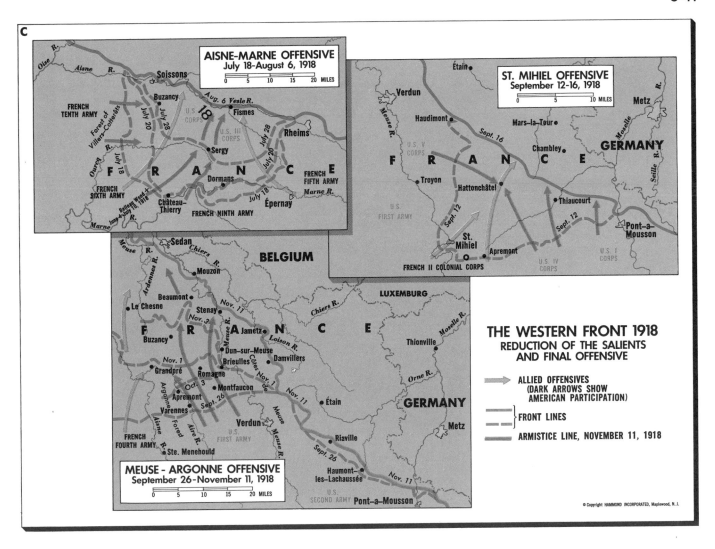

C

AISNE-MARNE OFFENSIVE
July 18-August 6, 1918
0 5 10 15 20 MILES

ST. MIHIEL OFFENSIVE
September 12-16, 1918
0 5 10 MILES

Oise R. · Aisne R. · Soissons · Buzancy · Aug. 6 Vesle R. · Fismes · July 28 · Rheims · FRENCH TENTH ARMY · Forest of Villers-Cotterêts · July 20 · July 28 · 18 · U.S. I CORPS · July 28 · July 20 · U.S. III CORPS · July 18 · Sergy · Ource R. · July 18 · F R A N C E · Dormans · FRENCH FIFTH ARMY · FRENCH SIXTH ARMY · Belleau Wood June 6-July 10, 1918 · Château-Thierry · July 18 · Épernay · Marne R. · FRENCH NINTH ARMY · Marne R.

Étain · Verdun · Mars-la-Tour · Metz · Haudimont · Chambley · GERMANY · Meuse R. · U.S. V CORPS · Sept. 16 · F R A N C E · Troyon · Hattonchâtel · Thiaucourt · U.S. FIRST ARMY · Sept. 12 · St. Mihiel · Apremont · Sept. 12 · Pont-à-Mousson · Moselle R. · Seille R. · FRENCH II COLONIAL CORPS · U.S. I CORPS · U.S. IV CORPS

Meuse R. · Sedan · Chiers R. · BELGIUM · Ardennes R. · Mouzon · LUXEMBURG · Beaumont · Nov. 11 · Le Chesne · Stenay · Nov. 3 · Chiers R. · Meuse R. · Jametz · F R A N C E · Buzancy · Loison R. · Dun-sur-Meuse · Damvillers · Thionville · Brieulles · Côtes de Meuse · Nov. 1 · Moselle R. · Nov. 1 · Grandpré · Romagne · Oct. 3 · Montfaucon · Nov. 11 · Étain · Apremont · Sept. 26 · Orne R. · GERMANY · Varennes · Argonne Forest · Verdun · Metz · FRENCH FOURTH ARMY · Aire R. · U.S. FIRST ARMY · Meuse R. · Riaville · Aisne R. · Ste. Menehould · Sept. 26 · Haumont-les-Lachaussée · Nov. 11 · U.S. SECOND ARMY · Pont-à-Mousson

MEUSE - ARGONNE OFFENSIVE
September 26-November 11, 1918
0 5 10 15 20 MILES

THE WESTERN FRONT 1918
REDUCTION OF THE SALIENTS
AND FINAL OFFENSIVE

→ ALLIED OFFENSIVES
(DARK ARROWS SHOW
AMERICAN PARTICIPATION)

‒ ‒ } FRONT LINES

━━ ARMISTICE LINE, NOVEMBER 11, 1918

© Copyright HAMMOND INCORPORATED, Maplewood, N. J.

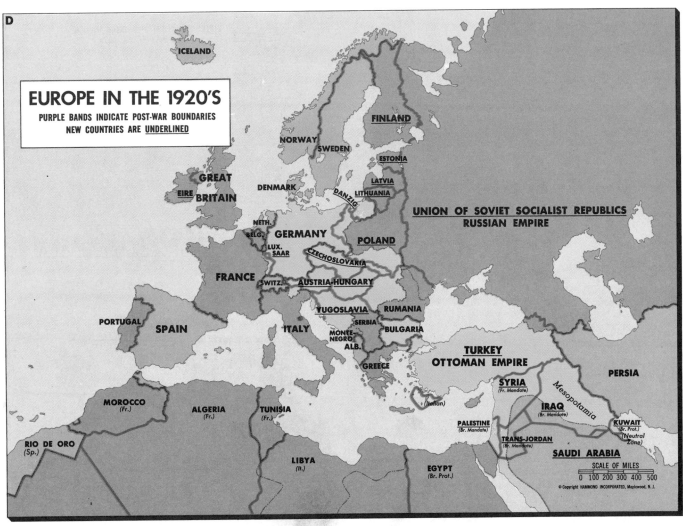

D

EUROPE IN THE 1920'S
PURPLE BANDS INDICATE POST-WAR BOUNDARIES
NEW COUNTRIES ARE <u>UNDERLINED</u>

ICELAND

<u>FINLAND</u> · NORWAY · SWEDEN · <u>ESTONIA</u> · <u>LATVIA</u> · <u>LITHUANIA</u> · <u>DANZIG</u>
<u>EIRE</u> · GREAT BRITAIN · DENMARK
NETH. · BELG. · GERMANY · <u>POLAND</u> · UNION OF SOVIET SOCIALIST REPUBLICS
LUX. · <u>SAAR</u> · <u>CZECHOSLOVAKIA</u> · RUSSIAN EMPIRE
FRANCE · SWITZ. · <u>AUSTRIA-HUNGARY</u>
<u>YUGOSLAVIA</u> · RUMANIA
PORTUGAL · SPAIN · ITALY · SERBIA · BULGARIA
MONTE-NEGRO · ALB.
GREECE · TURKEY · OTTOMAN EMPIRE · PERSIA
<u>SYRIA</u> (Fr. Mandate) · Mesopotamia
(Italian) · <u>IRAQ</u> (Br. Mandate) · <u>KUWAIT</u> (Br. Prot.) (Neutral Zone)
MOROCCO (Fr.) · ALGERIA (Fr.) · TUNISIA (Fr.) · <u>PALESTINE</u> (Br. Mandate) · <u>TRANS-JORDAN</u> (Br. Mandate) · <u>SAUDI ARABIA</u>
RIO DE ORO (Sp.) · LIBYA (It.) · EGYPT (Br. Prot.)

SCALE OF MILES
0 100 200 300 400 500

© Copyright HAMMOND INCORPORATED, Maplewood, N. J.

A

THE GREAT DEPRESSION

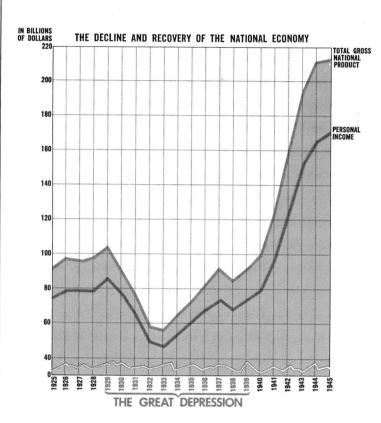

IN BILLIONS OF DOLLARS

THE DECLINE AND RECOVERY OF THE NATIONAL ECONOMY

TOTAL GROSS NATIONAL PRODUCT

PERSONAL INCOME

THE GREAT DEPRESSION

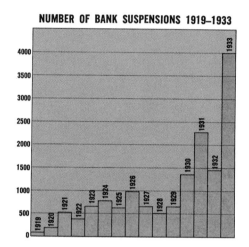

NUMBER OF BANK SUSPENSIONS 1919–1933

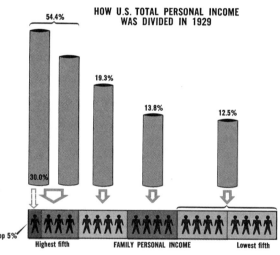

HOW U.S. TOTAL PERSONAL INCOME WAS DIVIDED IN 1929

54.4%

30.0%

19.3%

13.8%

12.5%

Top 5%

Highest fifth   FAMILY PERSONAL INCOME   Lowest fifth

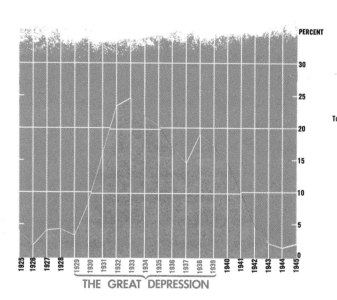

UNEMPLOYMENT

THE UNEMPLOYED AS A PERCENT OF THE CIVILIAN LABOR FORCE

PERCENT

THE GREAT DEPRESSION

HOURS

HOURS WORKED IN MANUFACTURING (1925–1945)
(WEEKLY AVERAGE)

Source: *Historical Statistics of the United States*

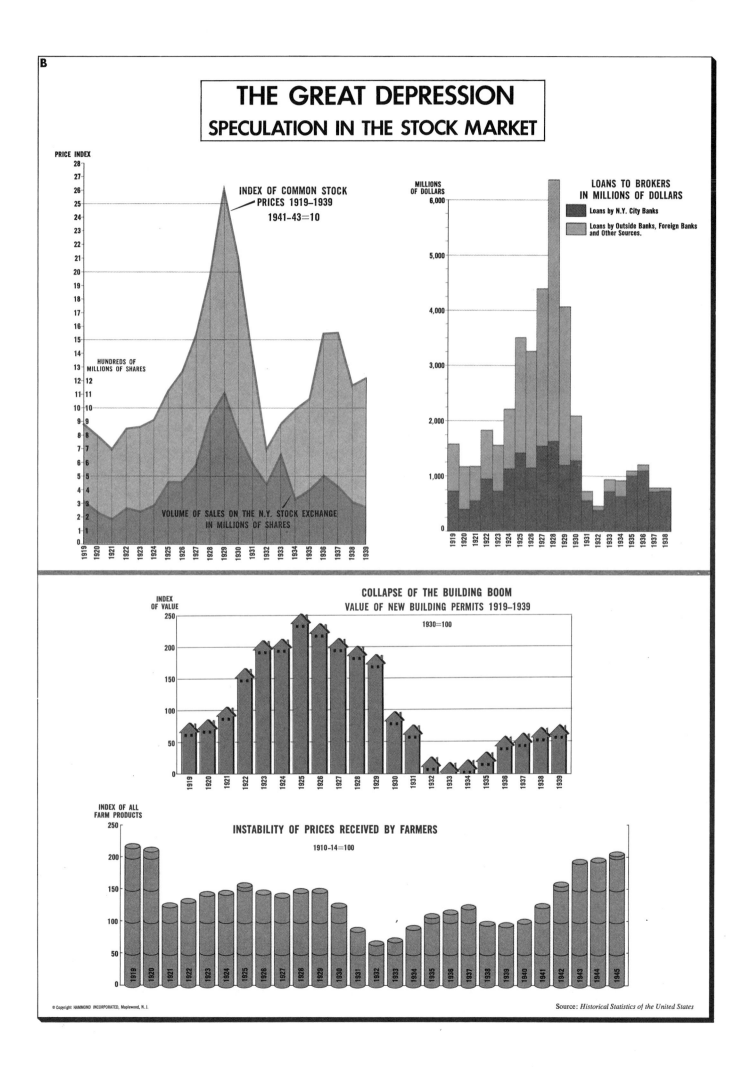

THE GREAT DEPRESSION
SPECULATION IN THE STOCK MARKET

INDEX OF COMMON STOCK PRICES 1919–1939 1941–43=10

VOLUME OF SALES ON THE N.Y. STOCK EXCHANGE IN MILLIONS OF SHARES

LOANS TO BROKERS IN MILLIONS OF DOLLARS
- Loans by N.Y. City Banks
- Loans by Outside Banks, Foreign Banks and Other Sources.

COLLAPSE OF THE BUILDING BOOM
VALUE OF NEW BUILDING PERMITS 1919–1939 1930=100

INSTABILITY OF PRICES RECEIVED BY FARMERS 1910–14=100

Source: *Historical Statistics of the United States*

A

CONSERVATION OF NATURAL RESOURCES
THE PUBLIC DOMAIN

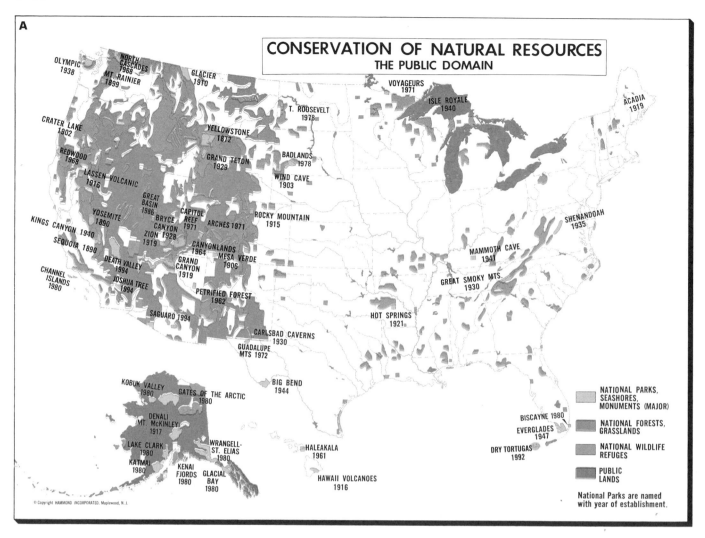

OLYMPIC 1938
NORTH CASCADES 1968
MT. RAINIER 1899
GLACIER 1910
VOYAGEURS 1971
ISLE ROYALE 1940
ACADIA 1919
CRATER LAKE 1902
T. ROOSEVELT 1978
REDWOOD 1968
YELLOWSTONE 1872
BADLANDS 1978
LASSEN VOLCANIC 1916
GRAND TETON 1929
WIND CAVE 1903
SHENANDOAH 1935
GREAT BASIN 1986
YOSEMITE 1890
BRYCE CANYON 1971
CAPITOL REEF 1971
ARCHES 1971
ROCKY MOUNTAIN 1915
KINGS CANYON 1940
ZION 1919
CANYONLANDS 1964
MAMMOTH CAVE 1941
SEQUOIA 1890
DEATH VALLEY 1994
GRAND CANYON 1919
MESA VERDE 1906
GREAT SMOKY MTS. 1930
CHANNEL ISLANDS 1980
JOSHUA TREE 1994
PETRIFIED FOREST 1962
SAGUARO 1994
HOT SPRINGS 1921
CARLSBAD CAVERNS 1930
GUADALUPE MTS 1972
BIG BEND 1944
KOBUK VALLEY 1980
GATES OF THE ARCTIC 1980
BISCAYNE 1980
EVERGLADES 1947
DENALI (MT. McKINLEY) 1917
DRY TORTUGAS 1992
LAKE CLARK 1980
WRANGELL-ST. ELIAS 1980
KATMAI 1980
HALEAKALA 1961
KENAI FJORDS 1980
GLACIAL BAY 1980
HAWAII VOLCANOES 1916

© Copyright HAMMOND INCORPORATED, Maplewood, N.J.

- NATIONAL PARKS, SEASHORES, MONUMENTS (MAJOR)
- NATIONAL FORESTS, GRASSLANDS
- NATIONAL WILDLIFE REFUGES
- PUBLIC LANDS

National Parks are named with year of establishment.

B

CONSERVATION OF NATURAL RESOURCES
WATER CONTROL

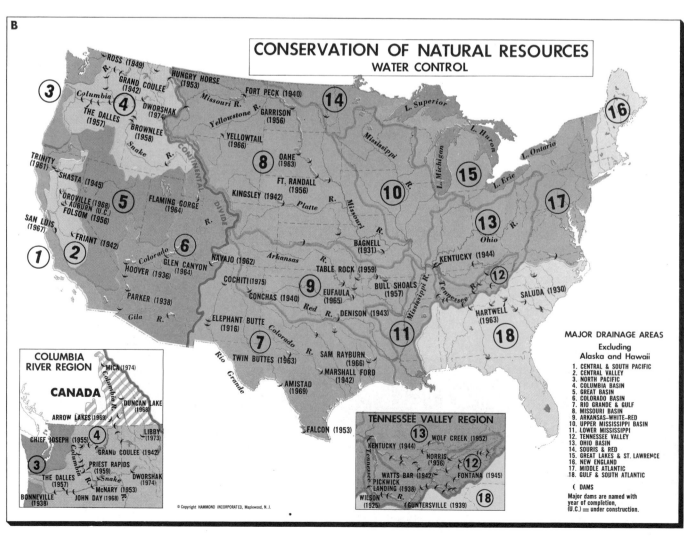

ROSS (1949)
GRAND COULEE (1942)
HUNGRY HORSE (1953)
FORT PECK (1940)
DWORSHAK (1974)
THE DALLES (1957)
GARRISON (1956)
BROWNLEE (1958)
YELLOWTAIL (1966)
TRINITY (1961)
SHASTA (1945)
OAHE (1963)
FT. RANDALL (1956)
OROVILLE (1968)
AUBURN (U.C.)
FLAMING GORGE (1964)
KINGSLEY (1942)
FOLSOM (1956)
SAN LUIS (1967)
FRIANT (1942)
BAGNELL (1931)
KENTUCKY (1944)
GLEN CANYON (1964)
NAVAJO (1962)
TABLE ROCK (1959)
HOOVER (1936)
COCHITI (1975)
EUFAULA (1965)
BULL SHOALS (1957)
SALUDA (1930)
PARKER (1938)
CONCHAS (1940)
DENISON (1943)
HARTWELL (1963)
ELEPHANT BUTTE (1916)
SAM RAYBURN (1966)
TWIN BUTTES (1963)
MARSHALL FORD (1942)
AMISTAD (1969)
FALCON (1953)

Columbia
Missouri R.
Yellowstone R.
Snake R.
CONTINENTAL DIVIDE
Platte R.
Missouri R.
Mississippi R.
L. Superior
L. Huron
L. Michigan
L. Ontario
L. Erie
Colorado R.
Arkansas R.
Ohio R.
Tennessee R.
Red R.
Colorado R.
Rio Grande
Gila R.
Mississippi R.

COLUMBIA RIVER REGION

MICA (1974)
CANADA
DUNCAN LAKE (1968)
ARROW LAKES (1969)
Columbia R.
LIBBY (1973)
CHIEF JOSEPH (1955)
GRAND COULEE (1942)
PRIEST RAPIDS (1959)
THE DALLES (1957)
Snake R.
DWORSHAK (1974)
McNARY (1953)
BONNEVILLE (1938)
JOHN DAY (1968)

© Copyright HAMMOND INCORPORATED, Maplewood, N.J.

TENNESSEE VALLEY REGION

WOLF CREEK (1952)
KENTUCKY (1944)
NORRIS (1936)
FONTANA (1945)
WATTS BAR (1942)
PICKWICK LANDING (1938)
WILSON (1925)
Tennessee R.
GUNTERSVILLE (1939)

MAJOR DRAINAGE AREAS
Excluding Alaska and Hawaii

1. CENTRAL & SOUTH PACIFIC
2. CENTRAL VALLEY
3. NORTH PACIFIC
4. COLUMBIA BASIN
5. GREAT BASIN
6. COLORADO BASIN
7. RIO GRANDE & GULF
8. MISSOURI BASIN
9. ARKANSAS–WHITE–RED
10. UPPER MISSISSIPPI BASIN
11. LOWER MISSISSIPPI
12. TENNESSEE VALLEY
13. OHIO BASIN
14. SOURIS & RED
15. GREAT LAKES & ST. LAWRENCE
16. NEW ENGLAND
17. MIDDLE ATLANTIC
18. GULF & SOUTH ATLANTIC

(DAMS

Major dams are named with year of completion.
(U.C.) = under construction.

C

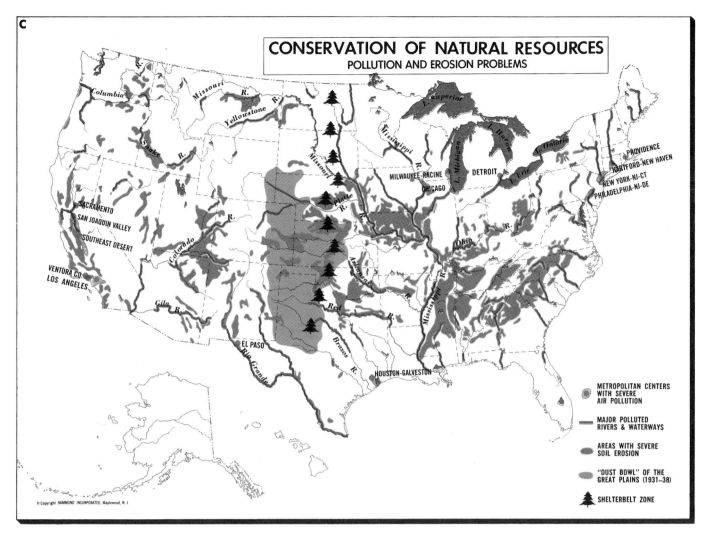

CONSERVATION OF NATURAL RESOURCES
POLLUTION AND EROSION PROBLEMS

METROPOLITAN CENTERS WITH SEVERE AIR POLLUTION

MAJOR POLLUTED RIVERS & WATERWAYS

AREAS WITH SEVERE SOIL EROSION

"DUST BOWL" OF THE GREAT PLAINS (1931–38)

SHELTERBELT ZONE

© Copyright HAMMOND INCORPORATED, Maplewood, N.J.

D

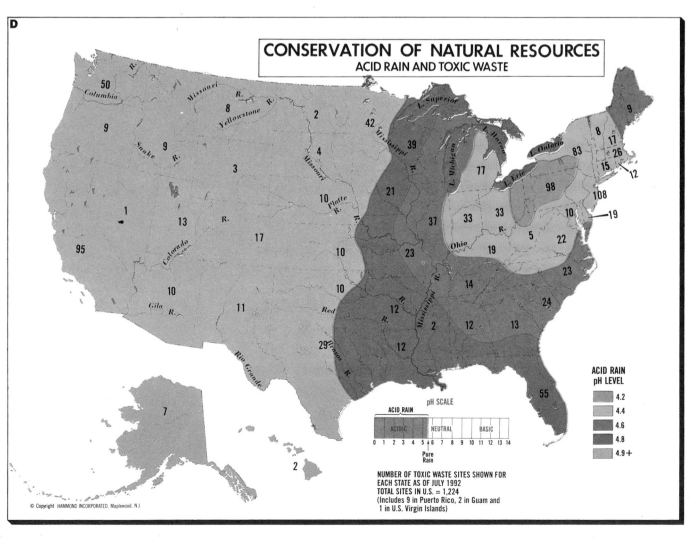

CONSERVATION OF NATURAL RESOURCES
ACID RAIN AND TOXIC WASTE

ACID RAIN pH LEVEL

4.2
4.4
4.6
4.8
4.9 +

pH SCALE

ACID RAIN

ACIDIC | NEUTRAL | BASIC

0 1 2 3 4 5 6 7 8 9 10 11 12 13 14

Pure Rain

NUMBER OF TOXIC WASTE SITES SHOWN FOR EACH STATE AS OF JULY 1992
TOTAL SITES IN U.S. = 1,224
(Includes 9 in Puerto Rico, 2 in Guam and 1 in U.S. Virgin Islands)

© Copyright HAMMOND INCORPORATED, Maplewood, N.J.

GERMAN EXPANSION 1935-1939*

SCALE OF MILES

0 100 200 300 400

Germany 1933

Area gained by Plebiscite 1935

Areas annexed 1938

Area annexed 1939

German Protectorates

*To Invasion of Poland Sept. 1, 1939

MEMEL To Germany 1939

Rhineland remilitarized 1936

BOHEMIA & MORAVIA German Protectorate and occupation 1939

SAAR To Germany 1935

SUDETENLAND To Germany 1938

SLOVAKIA German Protectorate 1939

AUSTRIA To Germany 1938

Civil War 1936–1939

© Copyright HAMMOND INCORPORATED, Maplewood, N.J.

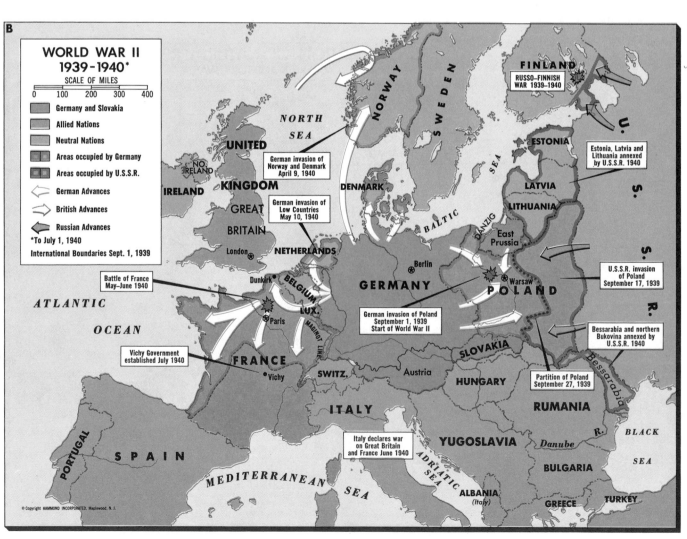

WORLD WAR II 1939-1940*

SCALE OF MILES

0 100 200 300 400

Germany and Slovakia

Allied Nations

Neutral Nations

Areas occupied by Germany

Areas occupied by U.S.S.R.

German Advances

British Advances

Russian Advances

*To July 1, 1940

International Boundaries Sept. 1, 1939

RUSSO–FINNISH WAR 1939–1940

German invasion of Norway and Denmark April 9, 1940

German invasion of Low Countries May 10, 1940

Estonia, Latvia and Lithuania annexed by U.S.S.R. 1940

Battle of France May–June 1940

U.S.S.R. invasion of Poland September 17, 1939

German invasion of Poland September 1, 1939 Start of World War II

Vichy Government established July 1940

Bessarabia and northern Bukovina annexed by U.S.S.R. 1940

Partition of Poland September 27, 1939

Italy declares war on Great Britain and France June 1940

© Copyright HAMMOND INCORPORATED, Maplewood, N.J.

C

WORLD WAR II EUROPEAN THEATER 1940-1942

- Allied Nations and Allied controlled Nations
- Axis Powers and Axis controlled Nations
- Neutral Nations
- Vichy France; Vichy controlled Areas (later to Allies)
- Areas occupied by Axis

German Air Strikes

Famous Battles or Sieges

German Advances

Allied Advances

Western Front

Eastern Front

British occupation 1940
U.S. occupation 1941
Independent 1944

ICELAND

SUPPLY ROUTE FROM U.S. & BRITISH COMMONWEALTH

NORWEGIAN SEA

Murmansk

NORTH SEA

UNITED IRELAND KINGDOM

SUPPLY ROUTE FROM U.S.

German U-boat Blockade

DENMARK

London

NETH.

BELG.

LUX.

Berlin

GERMANY

Paris

VICHY FRANCE

SWITZ.

Austria

POLAND

SLOVAKIA

HUNGARY

RUMANIA

YUGOSLAVIA

BULGARIA

Leningrad

EST.

LATVIA

LITH.

Moscow

UNION OF SOVIET SOCIALIST REPUBLICS

Ukraine

Stalingrad

CASPIAN SEA

ATLANTIC OCEAN

PORTUGAL

SPAIN

ITALY

Corsica

Rome

Sardinia

ALB. (It.)

GREECE

MEDITERRANEAN

Gibraltar (Br.)

Sp. Mor.

Casablanca

Oran

Algiers

Tunis

Sicily

Malta (Br.)

Crete

BLACK SEA

TURKEY
Neutral until Feb. 1945

Axis influence removed after British and Russian invasion 1941

ALLIED SUPPLY ROUTE TO U.S.S.R.

IRAN

IRAN

SYRIA (Fr.)

IRAQ

Cyprus (Br.)

Canary Is. (Sp.)

MOROCCO (Fr.)

RIO DE ORO (Sp.)

ALGERIA (Fr.)

TUNISIA (Fr.)

Tripoli

El Alamein

Cairo

PALESTINE (Br. Mandate)

TRANS-JORDAN (Br. Mandate)

Pro-Axis government removed by British 1941

SAUDI ARABIA
Neutral until Mar. 1945

Persian Gulf

SCALE OF MILES
0 100 200 300 400 500

LIBYA (It.)

EGYPT

©Copyright HAMMOND INCORPORATED, Maplewood, N.J.

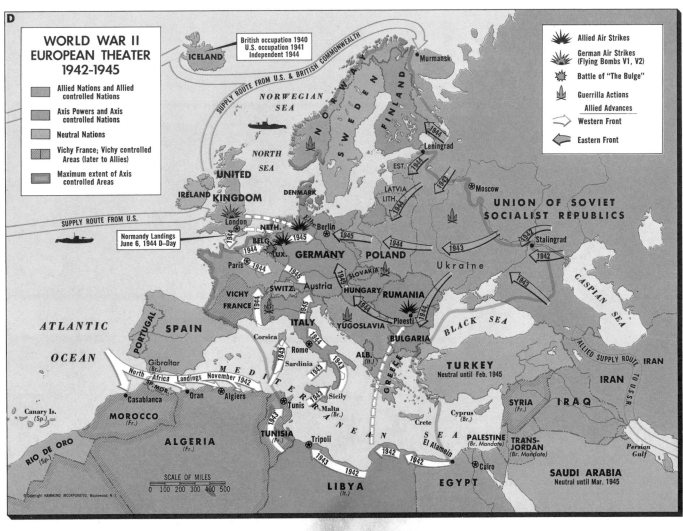

D

WORLD WAR II EUROPEAN THEATER 1942-1945

- Allied Nations and Allied controlled Nations
- Axis Powers and Axis controlled Nations
- Neutral Nations
- Vichy France; Vichy controlled Areas (later to Allies)
- Maximum extent of Axis controlled Areas

Allied Air Strikes

German Air Strikes (Flying Bombs V1, V2)

Battle of "The Bulge"

Guerrilla Actions

Allied Advances

Western Front

Eastern Front

British occupation 1940
U.S. occupation 1941
Independent 1944

ICELAND

SUPPLY ROUTE FROM U.S. & BRITISH COMMONWEALTH

NORWEGIAN SEA

Murmansk

NORTH SEA

UNITED IRELAND KINGDOM

SUPPLY ROUTE FROM U.S.

Normandy Landings June 6, 1944 D-Day

London

NETH.

BELG.

Lux.

Berlin

GERMANY

Paris

VICHY FRANCE

SWITZ.

Austria

POLAND

SLOVAKIA

HUNGARY

RUMANIA

Ploesti

YUGOSLAVIA

BULGARIA

Leningrad

EST.

LATVIA

LITH.

Moscow

UNION OF SOVIET SOCIALIST REPUBLICS

Ukraine

Stalingrad

CASPIAN SEA

ATLANTIC OCEAN

PORTUGAL

SPAIN

ITALY

Corsica

Rome

Sardinia

ALB. (It.)

GREECE

North Africa Landings November 1942

Gibraltar (Br.)

Sp. Mor.

Casablanca

Oran

Algiers

Tunis

Sicily

Malta (Br.)

Crete

MEDITERRANEAN SEA

BLACK SEA

TURKEY
Neutral until Feb. 1945

ALLIED SUPPLY ROUTE TO U.S.S.R.

IRAN

IRAN

SYRIA (Fr.)

IRAQ

Cyprus (Br.)

Canary Is. (Sp.)

MOROCCO (Fr.)

RIO DE ORO (Sp.)

ALGERIA (Fr.)

TUNISIA (Fr.)

Tripoli

El Alamein

Cairo

PALESTINE (Br. Mandate)

TRANS-JORDAN (Br. Mandate)

SAUDI ARABIA
Neutral until Mar. 1945

Persian Gulf

SCALE OF MILES
0 100 200 300 400 500

LIBYA (It.)

EGYPT

©Copyright HAMMOND INCORPORATED, Maplewood, N.J.

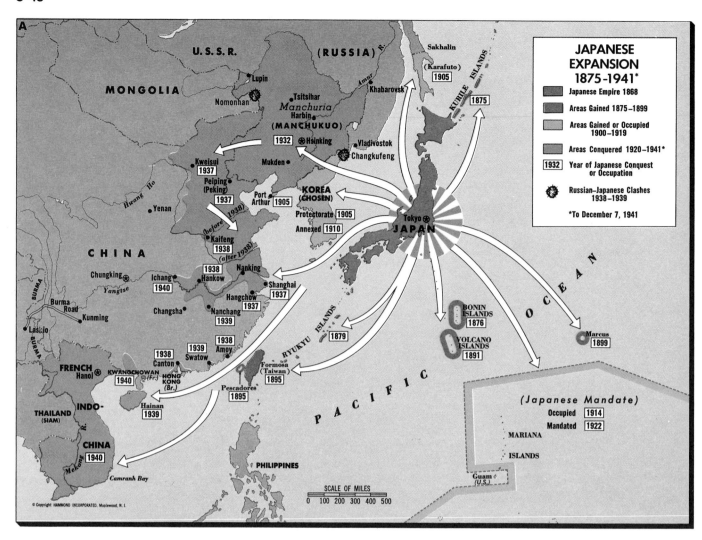

JAPANESE EXPANSION 1875–1941*

- Japanese Empire 1868
- Areas Gained 1875–1899
- Areas Gained or Occupied 1900–1919
- Areas Conquered 1920–1941*
- 1932 Year of Japanese Conquest or Occupation
- Russian–Japanese Clashes 1938–1939

*To December 7, 1941

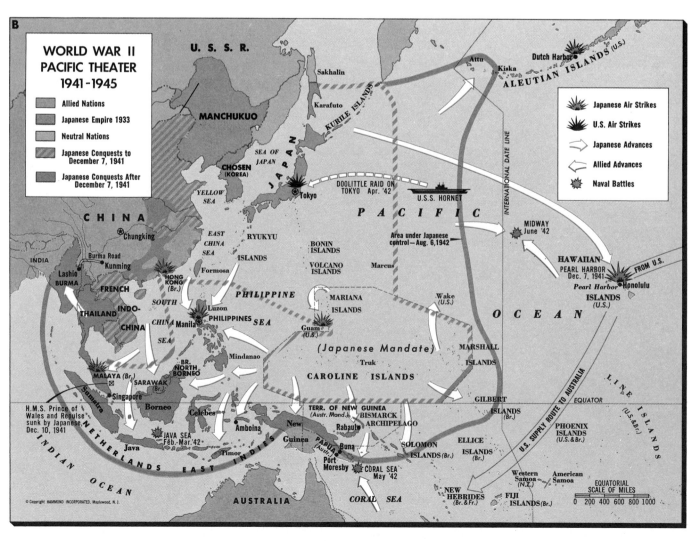

WORLD WAR II PACIFIC THEATER 1941–1945

- Allied Nations
- Japanese Empire 1933
- Neutral Nations
- Japanese Conquests to December 7, 1941
- Japanese Conquests After December 7, 1941

- Japanese Air Strikes
- U.S. Air Strikes
- Japanese Advances
- Allied Advances
- Naval Battles

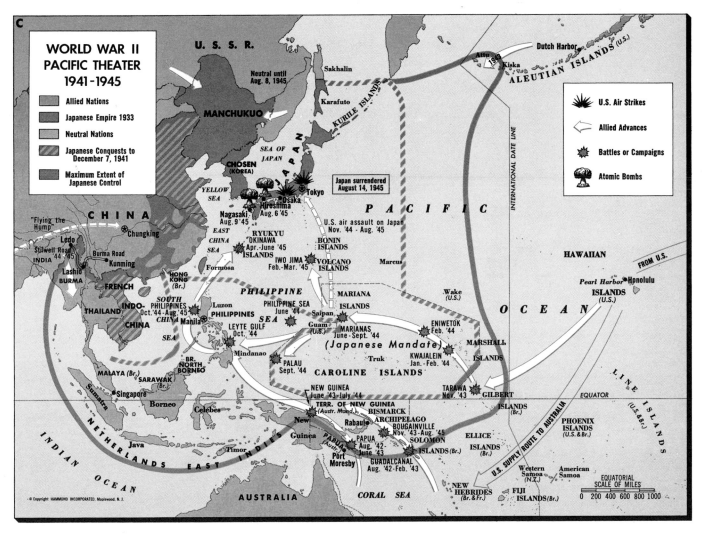

C

WORLD WAR II PACIFIC THEATER 1941-1945

- Allied Nations
- Japanese Empire 1933
- Neutral Nations
- Japanese Conquests to December 7, 1941
- Maximum Extent of Japanese Control

- ✷ U.S. Air Strikes
- ⇦ Allied Advances
- ✺ Battles or Campaigns
- ☁ Atomic Bombs

Japan surrendered August 14, 1945

U. S. S. R.

Dutch Harbor (U.S.)
ALEUTIAN ISLANDS (U.S.)
Attu 1943
Kiska

Sakhalin
Karafuto
MANCHUKUO
KURILE ISLANDS
Neutral until Aug. 8, 1945

SEA OF JAPAN
JAPAN
CHOSEN (KOREA)
YELLOW SEA
Tokyo
Osaka
Hiroshima Aug. 6 '45
Nagasaki Aug. 9 '45

INTERNATIONAL DATE LINE

PACIFIC

"Flying the Hump"
CHINA
Chungking
Ledo
Stilwell Road '44-'45
INDIA
Burma Road
Kunming
Lashio
BURMA

EAST CHINA SEA
RYUKYU OKINAWA Apr.-June '45 ISLANDS
Formosa
HONG KONG (Br.)
U.S. air assault on Japan Nov. '44 - Aug. '45

BONIN ISLANDS
IWO JIMA Feb.-Mar. '45
VOLCANO ISLANDS
Marcus

HAWAIIAN

FROM U.S.

FRENCH
THAILAND
INDO-CHINA
SOUTH PHILIPPINES Oct. '44-Aug. '45
PHILIPPINE SEA June '44
PHILIPPINES
Manila
LEYTE GULF Oct. '44
SOUTH CHINA SEA
Luzon

Saipan
MARIANA ISLANDS
Guam (U.S.)
MARIANAS June-Sept. '44
(Japanese Mandate)
Wake (U.S.)
Pearl Harbor Honolulu
ISLANDS (U.S.)

OCEAN

MALAYA (Br.)
SARAWAK (Br.)
Singapore
Sumatra
Borneo
BR. NORTH BORNEO
Celebes
Mindanao
Java
Timor

PALAU Sept. '44
Truk
KWAJALEIN Jan.-Feb. '44
ENIWETOK Feb. '44
MARSHALL ISLANDS

CAROLINE ISLANDS

TARAWA Nov. '43
GILBERT ISLANDS (Br.)

EQUATOR

LINE ISLANDS (U.S.&Br.)

NETHERLANDS EAST INDIES

INDIAN OCEAN

NEW GUINEA June '43-July '44
TERR. OF NEW GUINEA (Austr. Mand.)
New Guinea
PAPUA (Austr.)
Port Moresby
GUADALCANAL Aug. '42-Feb. '43
PAPUA Aug. '42-June '43
Rabaul
BISMARCK ARCHIPELAGO
BOUGAINVILLE Nov. '43-Aug. '45
SOLOMON ISLANDS (Br.)

ELLICE ISLANDS (Br.)

U.S. SUPPLY ROUTE TO AUSTRALIA

PHOENIX ISLANDS (U.S. & Br.)

AUSTRALIA

CORAL SEA

NEW HEBRIDES (Br. & Fr.)
FIJI ISLANDS (Br.)
Western Samoa (N.Z.)
American Samoa

EQUATORIAL SCALE OF MILES
0 200 400 600 800 1000

© Copyright HAMMOND INCORPORATED, Maplewood, N.J.

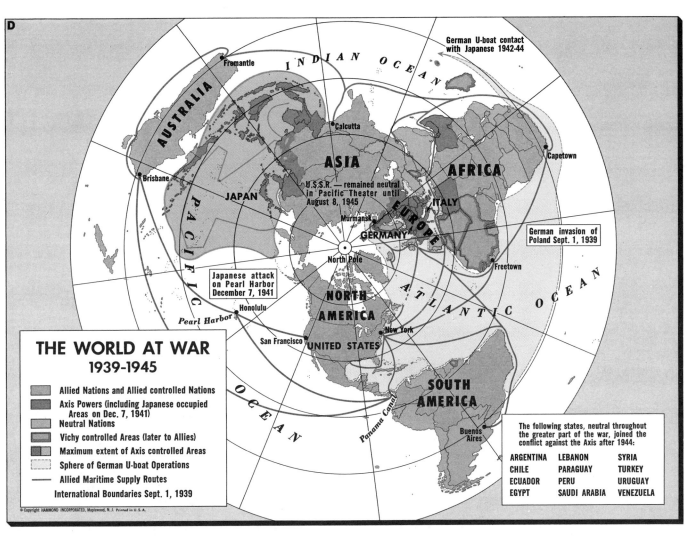

D

THE WORLD AT WAR 1939-1945

- Allied Nations and Allied controlled Nations
- Axis Powers (including Japanese occupied Areas on Dec. 7, 1941)
- Neutral Nations
- Vichy controlled Areas (later to Allies)
- Maximum extent of Axis controlled Areas
- Sphere of German U-boat Operations
- Allied Maritime Supply Routes
- International Boundaries Sept. 1, 1939

German U-boat contact with Japanese 1942-44

German invasion of Poland Sept. 1, 1939

Japanese attack on Pearl Harbor December 7, 1941

U.S.S.R. — remained neutral in Pacific Theater until August 8, 1945

Fremantle
INDIAN OCEAN
AUSTRALIA
Calcutta
Capetown
Brisbane
PACIFIC
ASIA
AFRICA
JAPAN
EUROPE
ITALY
Murmansk
GERMANY
Freetown
North Pole
ATLANTIC OCEAN
NORTH AMERICA
Honolulu
Pearl Harbor
San Francisco
UNITED STATES
New York
SOUTH AMERICA
Panama Canal
Buenos Aires
OCEAN

The following states, neutral throughout the greater part of the war, joined the conflict against the Axis after 1944:

ARGENTINA	LEBANON	SYRIA
CHILE	PARAGUAY	TURKEY
ECUADOR	PERU	URUGUAY
EGYPT	SAUDI ARABIA	VENEZUELA

© Copyright HAMMOND INCORPORATED, Maplewood, N.J. Printed in U.S.A.

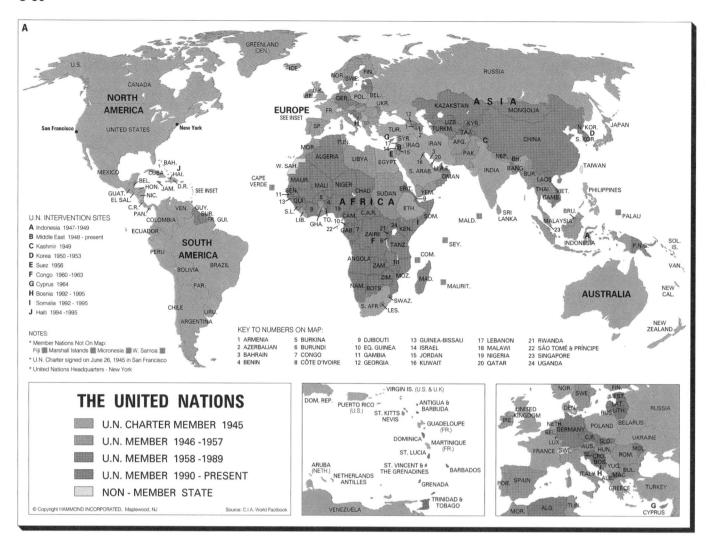

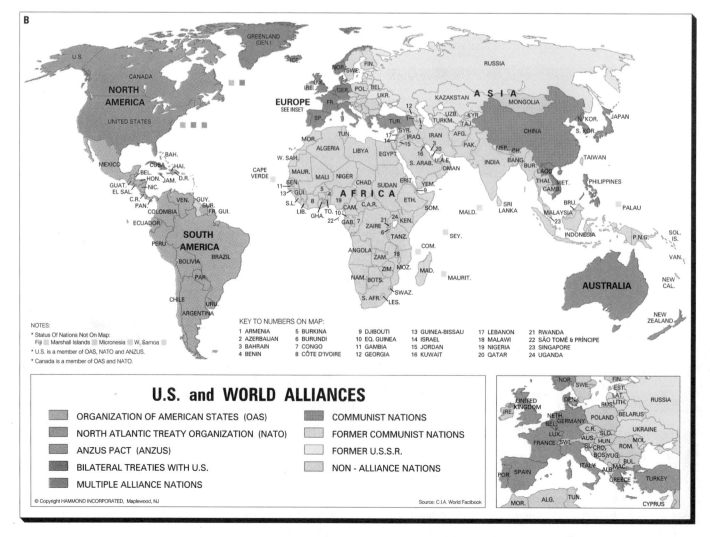

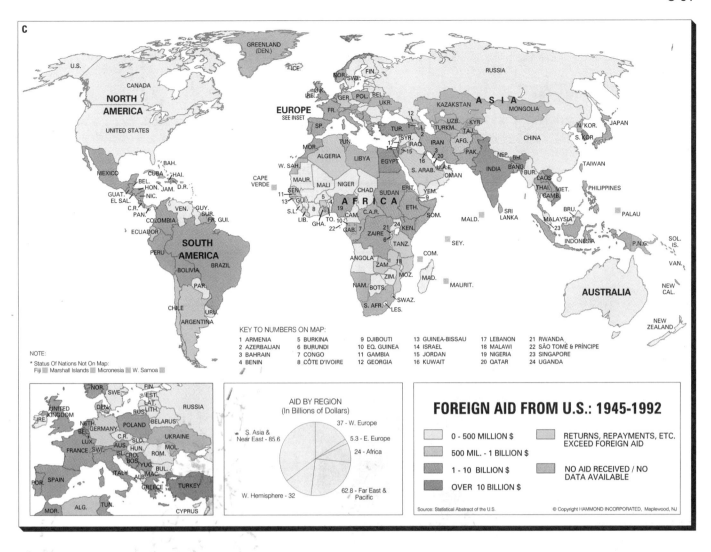

C

KEY TO NUMBERS ON MAP:

1 ARMENIA	5 BURKINA	9 DJIBOUTI
2 AZERBAIJAN	6 BURUNDI	10 EQ. GUINEA
3 BAHRAIN	7 CONGO	11 GAMBIA
4 BENIN	8 CÔTE D'IVOIRE	12 GEORGIA

13 GUINEA-BISSAU	17 LEBANON	21 RWANDA
14 ISRAEL	18 MALAWI	22 SÃO TOMÉ & PRÍNCIPE
15 JORDAN	19 NIGERIA	23 SINGAPORE
16 KUWAIT	20 QATAR	24 UGANDA

NOTE:
* Status Of Nations Not On Map:
Fiji ▨ Marshall Islands ▨ Micronesia ▨ W. Samoa ▨

AID BY REGION
(In Billions of Dollars)

37 - W. Europe
5.3 - E. Europe
24 - Africa
62.8 - Far East & Pacific
W. Hemisphere - 32
S. Asia & Near East - 85.6

FOREIGN AID FROM U.S.: 1945-1992

▢ 0 - 500 MILLION $
▢ 500 MIL. - 1 BILLION $
▢ 1 - 10 BILLION $
▢ OVER 10 BILLION $
▢ RETURNS, REPAYMENTS, ETC. EXCEED FOREIGN AID
▢ NO AID RECEIVED / NO DATA AVAILABLE

Source: Statistical Abstract of the U.S.
© Copyright HAMMOND INCORPORATED, Maplewood, NJ

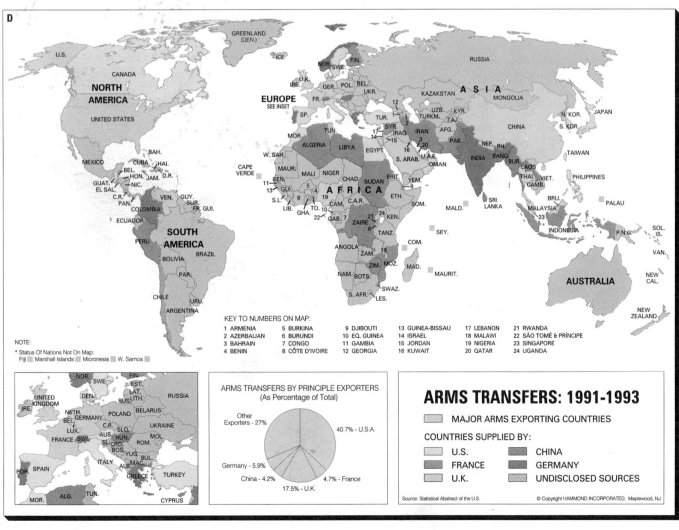

D

KEY TO NUMBERS ON MAP:

1 ARMENIA	5 BURKINA	9 DJIBOUTI
2 AZERBAIJAN	6 BURUNDI	10 EQ. GUINEA
3 BAHRAIN	7 CONGO	11 GAMBIA
4 BENIN	8 CÔTE D'IVOIRE	12 GEORGIA

13 GUINEA-BISSAU	17 LEBANON	21 RWANDA
14 ISRAEL	18 MALAWI	22 SÃO TOMÉ & PRÍNCIPE
15 JORDAN	19 NIGERIA	23 SINGAPORE
16 KUWAIT	20 QATAR	24 UGANDA

NOTE:
* Status Of Nations Not On Map:
Fiji ▨ Marshall Islands ▨ Micronesia ▨ W. Samoa ▨

ARMS TRANSFERS BY PRINCIPLE EXPORTERS
(As Percentage of Total)

Other Exporters - 27%
40.7% - U.S.A.
4.7% - France
17.5% - U.K.
China - 4.2%
Germany - 5.9%

ARMS TRANSFERS: 1991-1993

▨ MAJOR ARMS EXPORTING COUNTRIES

COUNTRIES SUPPLIED BY:

▢ U.S.	▢ CHINA
▢ FRANCE	▢ GERMANY
▢ U.K.	▨ UNDISCLOSED SOURCES

Source: Statistical Abstract of the U.S.
© Copyright HAMMOND INCORPORATED, Maplewood, NJ

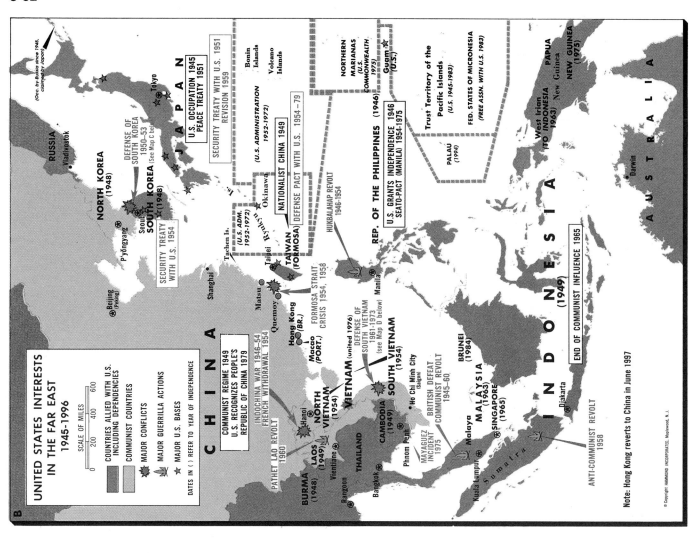

B

UNITED STATES INTERESTS IN THE FAR EAST 1945-1996

SCALE OF MILES

0   200   400   600

COUNTRIES ALLIED WITH U.S. INCLUDING DEPENDENCIES

COMMUNIST COUNTRIES

✺ MAJOR CONFLICTS

⚔ MAJOR GUERRILLA ACTIONS

★ MAJOR U.S. BASES

DATES IN ( ) REFER TO YEAR OF INDEPENDENCE

RUSSIA
• Vladivostok

NORTH KOREA (1948)
⊗ Pyŏngyang

DEFENSE OF SOUTH KOREA 1950-53 (See Map C below)

Seoul • SOUTH KOREA ★ (1948)

SECURITY TREATY WITH U.S. 1954

⊗ Beijing (Peking)

Shanghai •

C H I N A

COMMUNIST REGIME 1949
U.S. RECOGNIZES PEOPLE'S REPUBLIC OF CHINA 1979

(Occ. by Russia since 1945, claimed by Japan)

Tokyo

J A P A N

U.S. OCCUPATION 1945 PEACE TREATY 1951

SECURITY TREATY WITH U.S. 1951 REVISION 1959

Bonin Islands

Volcano Islands

(U.S. ADMINISTRATION 1952-1972)

Okinawa (U.S. ADM. 1952-1972) Ryukyus

NORTHERN MARIANAS (U.S. COMMONWEALTH 1975)

Guam ★ (U.S.)

Trust Territory of the Pacific Islands (U.S. 1945-1983)

FED. STATES OF MICRONESIA (FREE ASSN. WITH U.S. 1983)

PALAU (1994)

West Irian TO INDONESIA 1963

New Guinea

PAPUA NEW GUINEA (1975)

• Darwin

A U S T R A L I A

Tachen Is. ⊛

NATIONALIST CHINA 1949

Taipei ⊛ TAIWAN (FORMOSA)

DEFENSE PACT WITH U.S. 1954-79

Matsu ✺ Quemoy ✺

FORMOSA STRAIT CRISIS 1954, 1958

Hong Kong (BR.)

Macao (PORT.)

HUKBALAHAP REVOLT 1946-1954

⚔ Manila

REP. OF THE PHILIPPINES (1946)

U.S. GRANTS INDEPENDENCE 1946 SEATO-PACT (MANILA) 1954-1975

INDOCHINA WAR 1946-54 FRENCH WITHDRAWAL 1954

PATHET LAO REVOLT 1960

Hanoi ✺ NORTH VIETNAM (1954)

VIETNAM (united 1976)

DEFENSE OF SOUTH VIETNAM 1961-1973 (See Map D below)

SOUTH VIETNAM (1954)

Ho Chi Minh City (Saigon) •

BRUNEI (1984)

MALAYSIA (1963)

I N D O N E S I A (1949)

END OF COMMUNIST INFLUENCE 1965

BURMA (1948)

LAOS (1949)
Vientiane •

THAILAND

Rangoon •

⊛ Bangkok

CAMBODIA (1949)

Phnom Penh •

MAYAGUEZ INCIDENT 1975

BRITISH DEFEAT COMMUNIST REVOLT 1945-60

Malaya ⊛ SINGAPORE (1965)

Kuala Lumpur • MALAYA

Sumatra

• Djakarta

ANTI-COMMUNIST REVOLT 1958

Note: Hong Kong reverts to China in June 1997

© Copyright HAMMOND INCORPORATED, Maplewood, N.J.

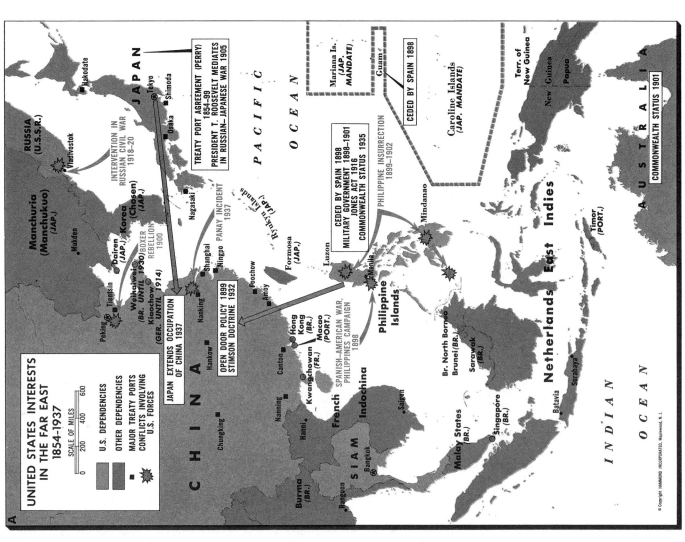

A

UNITED STATES INTERESTS IN THE FAR EAST 1854-1937

SCALE OF MILES

0   200   400   600

U.S. DEPENDENCIES

OTHER DEPENDENCIES

■ MAJOR TREATY PORTS

✺ CONFLICTS INVOLVING U.S. FORCES

RUSSIA (U.S.S.R.)
• Vladivostok

Manchuria (Manchukuo) (JAP.)

• Mukden

INTERVENTION IN RUSSIAN CIVIL WAR 1918-20

Korea (Chosen) (JAP.)

Peking ✺ • Tientsin

BOXER REBELLION 1900

Weihaiwei (BR. UNTIL 1930)

Dairen (JAP.)

Kiaochow (GER. UNTIL 1914)

Hakodate

J A P A N

⊛ Tokyo
Shimoda
Osaka ■
Nagasaki ■

TREATY PORT AGREEMENT (PERRY) 1854-99

PRESIDENT T. ROOSEVELT MEDIATES IN RUSSIAN-JAPANESE WAR 1905

PANAY INCIDENT 1937

Ryukyu Islands (JAP.)

P A C I F I C   O C E A N

Mariana Is. (JAP. MANDATE)

Guam ✺

CEDED BY SPAIN 1898

Caroline Islands (JAP. MANDATE)

Terr. of New Guinea

New Guinea Papua

A U S T R A L I A

COMMONWEALTH STATUS 1901

C H I N A

Nanking ■
Shanghai ■
Ningpo ■
Foochow ■
Amoy ■

OPEN DOOR POLICY 1899 STIMSON DOCTRINE 1932

JAPAN EXTENDS OCCUPATION OF CHINA 1937

Hankow ■

Nanning ■

Canton ■

Kwangchowan (FR.)

Hong Kong (BR.)

Macao (PORT.)

Chungking ■

Formosa (JAP.)

Luzon ✺

Manila ✺

Philippine Islands

SPANISH-AMERICAN WAR, PHILIPPINES CAMPAIGN 1898

CEDED BY SPAIN 1898 MILITARY GOVERNMENT 1898-1901 JONES ACT 1916 COMMONWEALTH STATUS 1935

PHILIPPINE INSURRECTION 1899-1902

Mindanao ✺

Br. North Borneo (BR.)

Brunei (BR.)
Sarawak (BR.)

Netherlands East Indies

Burma (BR.)

S I A M

Nanoi •
French Indochina

Saigon •

Bangkok •

Rangoon •

Maly States (BR.)

Singapore (BR.)

Timor (PORT.)

Batavia •

Surabaya •

I N D I A N   O C E A N

© Copyright HAMMOND INCORPORATED, Maplewood, N.J.

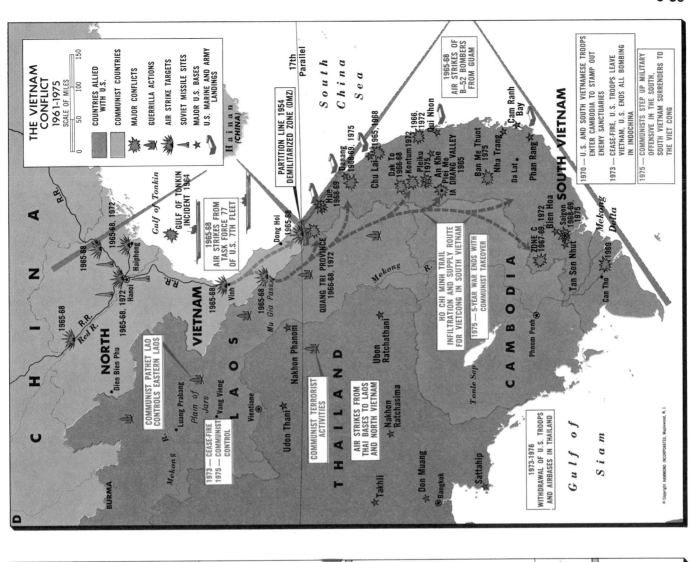

THE VIETNAM CONFLICT 1961-1975

SCALE OF MILES

COUNTRIES ALLIED WITH U.S.

COMMUNIST COUNTRIES

MAJOR CONFLICTS

GUERRILLA ACTIONS

AIR STRIKE TARGETS

SOVIET MISSILE SITES

MAJOR U.S. BASES

U.S. MARINE AND ARMY LANDINGS

C H I N A

R.R.

1965-68

R.R.

Red R.

1965-68, 1972

Haiphong

Hanoi

1965-68, 1972

Dien Bien Phu

NORTH VIETNAM

Vinh

1965-68

Mu Gia Pass

L A O S

Plain of Jars

Luang Prabang

Vang Vieng

Vientiane

Mekong R.

Udon Thani

Nakhon Phanom

Mekong

COMMUNIST PATHE LAO CONTROLS EASTERN LAOS

1973 — CEASE-FIRE
1975 — COMMUNIST CONTROL

COMMUNIST TERRORIST ACTIVITIES

AIR STRIKES FROM THAI BASES TO LAOS AND NORTH VIETNAM

T H A I L A N D

Nakhon Ratchasima

Ubon Ratchathani

Takhli

Don Muang

Bangkok

Sattahip

Gulf of Siam

Gulf of Tonkin

Gulf of Tonkin

GULF OF TONKIN INCIDENT 1964

1965-68 AIR STRIKES FROM TASK FORCE 77 OF U.S. 7TH FLEET

Hainan (CHINA)

PARTITION LINE 1954 DEMILITARIZED ZONE (DMZ)

17th Parallel

South China Sea

Dong Hoi

1965-68

Hue 1968-69

QUANG TRI PROVINCE 1966-68, 1972

Danang 1965, 1975

Chu Lai 1965, 1968

Dak To 1966-68

Kontum 1972, 1968

Pleiku 1966, 1972

Qui Nhon

An Khe

Plei Me 1975

IA DRANG VALLEY 1965

Ban Me Thuot 1975

Da Lat

Nha Trang

Phan Rang

Cam Ranh Bay

1965-68 AIR STRIKES OF B-52 BOMBERS FROM GUAM

SOUTH VIETNAM

HO CHI MINH TRAIL INFILTRATION AND SUPPLY ROUTE FOR VIETCONG IN SOUTH VIETNAM

1975 — 5-YEAR WAR ENDS WITH COMMUNIST TAKEOVER

C A M B O D I A

Phnom Penh

Tonle Sap

ZONE C 1967-69, 1972

Bien Hoa 1972

Saigon 1968-69, 1975

Tan Son Nhut

Can Tho

Mekong Delta

1969

1970 — U.S. AND SOUTH VIETNAMESE TROOPS ENTER CAMBODIA TO STAMP OUT ENEMY SANCTUARIES

1973 — CEASE-FIRE, U.S. TROOPS LEAVE VIETNAM, U.S. ENDS ALL BOMBING IN INDOCHINA

1975 — COMMUNISTS STEP UP MILITARY OFFENSIVE IN THE SOUTH, SOUTH VIETNAM SURRENDERS TO THE VIET CONG

1973-1976 WITHDRAWAL OF U.S. TROOPS AND AIRBASES IN THAILAND

© Copyright HAMMOND INCORPORATED, Maplewood, N.J.

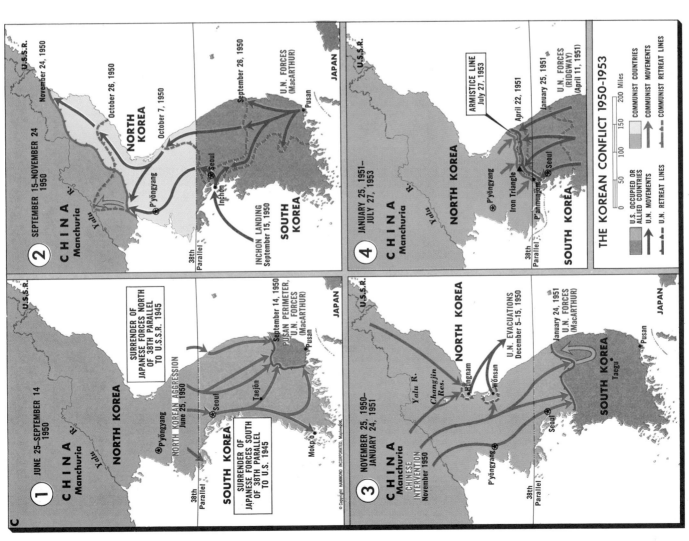

① JUNE 25–SEPTEMBER 14 1950

C H I N A
Manchuria

Yalu

U.S.S.R.

NORTH KOREA

Pʼyŏngyang

NORTH KOREAN AGGRESSION June 25, 1950

Seoul

Taejŏn

SURRENDER OF JAPANESE FORCES NORTH OF 38TH PARALLEL TO U.S.S.R. 1945

38th Parallel

SURRENDER OF JAPANESE FORCES SOUTH OF 38TH PARALLEL TO U.S. 1945

SOUTH KOREA

Mokpʼo

September 14, 1950 PUSAN PERIMETER, U.N. FORCES (MacARTHUR)

Pusan

JAPAN

© Copyright HAMMOND INCORPORATED, Maplewood

② SEPTEMBER 15–NOVEMBER 24 1950

C H I N A
Manchuria

Yalu

U.S.S.R.

November 24, 1950

October 26, 1950

NORTH KOREA

October 7, 1950

Pʼyŏngyang

Seoul

Inchŏn

INCHON LANDING September 15, 1950

38th Parallel

SOUTH KOREA

September 26, 1950

September 26, 1950

U.N. FORCES (MacARTHUR)

Pusan

JAPAN

③ NOVEMBER 25, 1950– JANUARY 24, 1951

C H I N A
Manchuria

Yalu R.

Chosin Res.

CHINESE INTERVENTION November 1950

U.S.S.R.

NORTH KOREA

Hŭngnam

Wŏnsan

U.N. EVACUATIONS December 5–15, 1950

Pʼyŏngyang

Seoul

January 24, 1951 U.N. FORCES (MacARTHUR)

38th Parallel

SOUTH KOREA

Taegu

Pusan

JAPAN

④ JANUARY 25, 1951– JULY 27, 1953

C H I N A
Manchuria

Yalu

U.S.S.R.

NORTH KOREA

ARMISTICE LINE July 27, 1953

April 22, 1951

Pʼyŏngyang

Iron Triangle

Pʼanmunjŏm

Seoul

38th Parallel

January 25, 1951 U.N. FORCES (RIDGWAY) (April 11, 1951)

SOUTH KOREA

THE KOREAN CONFLICT 1950-1953

U.S. OCCUPIED OR ALLIED COUNTRIES

U.N. MOVEMENTS

U.N. RETREAT LINES

COMMUNIST COUNTRIES

COMMUNIST MOVEMENTS

COMMUNIST RETREAT LINES

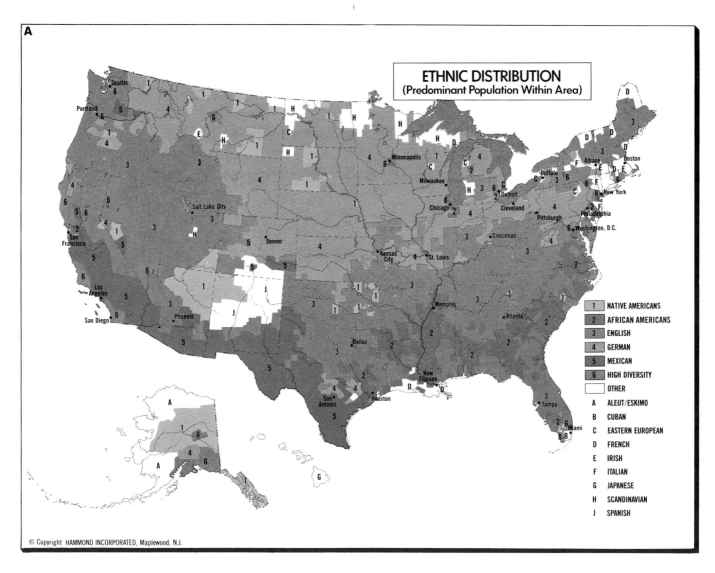

ETHNIC DISTRIBUTION
(Predominant Population Within Area)

1	NATIVE AMERICANS
2	AFRICAN AMERICANS
3	ENGLISH
4	GERMAN
5	MEXICAN
6	HIGH DIVERSITY
	OTHER
A	ALEUT/ESKIMO
B	CUBAN
C	EASTERN EUROPEAN
D	FRENCH
E	IRISH
F	ITALIAN
G	JAPANESE
H	SCANDINAVIAN
J	SPANISH

© Copyright HAMMOND INCORPORATED, Maplewood, N.J.

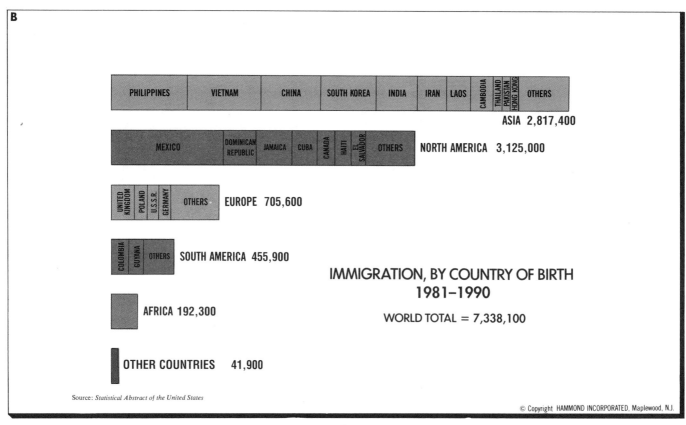

ASIA 2,817,400

NORTH AMERICA 3,125,000

EUROPE 705,600

SOUTH AMERICA 455,900

AFRICA 192,300

OTHER COUNTRIES 41,900

IMMIGRATION, BY COUNTRY OF BIRTH
1981–1990

WORLD TOTAL = 7,338,100

Source: *Statistical Abstract of the United States*

© Copyright HAMMOND INCORPORATED, Maplewood, N.J.

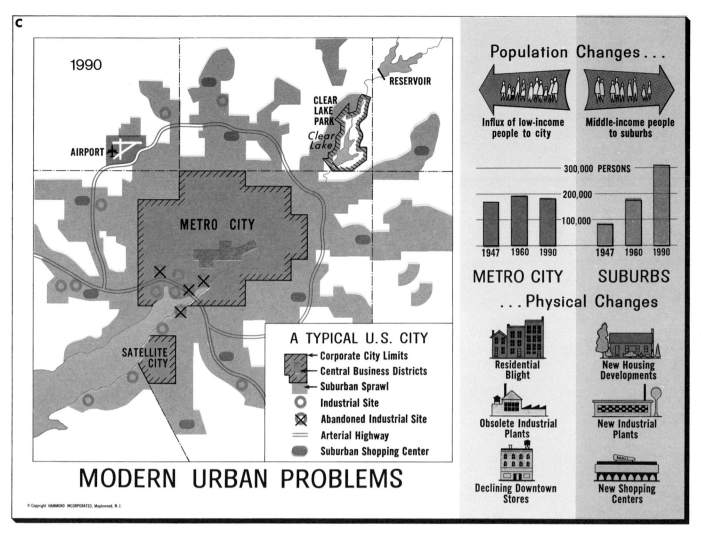

Population Changes...

Influx of low-income people to city

Middle-income people to suburbs

300,000 PERSONS

200,000

100,000

METRO CITY: 1947, 1960, 1990

SUBURBS: 1947, 1960, 1990

...Physical Changes

Residential Blight

New Housing Developments

Obsolete Industrial Plants

New Industrial Plants

Declining Downtown Stores

New Shopping Centers

1990

RESERVOIR

CLEAR LAKE PARK

Clear Lake

AIRPORT

METRO CITY

SATELLITE CITY

A TYPICAL U.S. CITY

- → Corporate City Limits
- — Central Business Districts
- ← Suburban Sprawl
- ○ Industrial Site
- ⊗ Abandoned Industrial Site
- ≡ Arterial Highway
- ⬭ Suburban Shopping Center

MODERN URBAN PROBLEMS

© Copyright HAMMOND INCORPORATED, Maplewood, N.J.

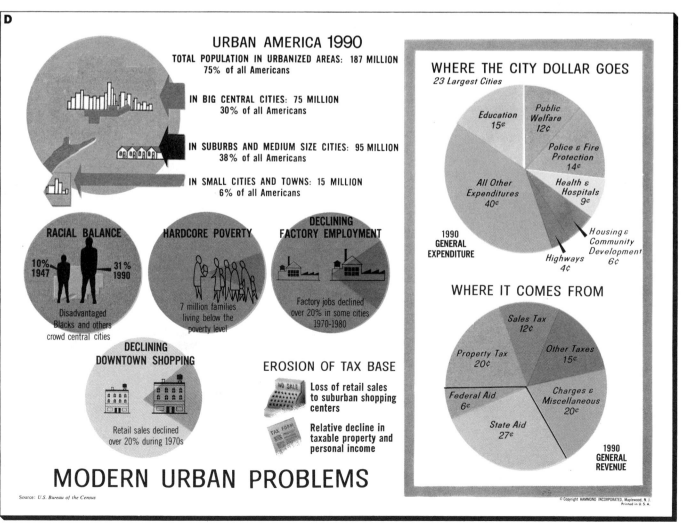

URBAN AMERICA 1990

TOTAL POPULATION IN URBANIZED AREAS: 187 MILLION
75% of all Americans

IN BIG CENTRAL CITIES: 75 MILLION
30% of all Americans

IN SUBURBS AND MEDIUM SIZE CITIES: 95 MILLION
38% of all Americans

IN SMALL CITIES AND TOWNS: 15 MILLION
6% of all Americans

RACIAL BALANCE
10% 1947 — 31% 1990
Disadvantaged Blacks and others crowd central cities

HARDCORE POVERTY
7 million families living below the poverty level

DECLINING FACTORY EMPLOYMENT
Factory jobs declined over 20% in some cities 1970-1980

DECLINING DOWNTOWN SHOPPING
Retail sales declined over 20% during 1970s

EROSION OF TAX BASE
Loss of retail sales to suburban shopping centers

Relative decline in taxable property and personal income

MODERN URBAN PROBLEMS

Source: U.S. Bureau of the Census

WHERE THE CITY DOLLAR GOES
23 Largest Cities

- Education 15¢
- Public Welfare 12¢
- Police & Fire Protection 14¢
- Health & Hospitals 9¢
- All Other Expenditures 40¢
- Housing & Community Development 6¢
- Highways 4¢

1990 GENERAL EXPENDITURE

WHERE IT COMES FROM

- Sales Tax 12¢
- Other Taxes 15¢
- Property Tax 20¢
- Charges & Miscellaneous 20¢
- Federal Aid 6¢
- State Aid 27¢

1990 GENERAL REVENUE

© Copyright HAMMOND INCORPORATED, Maplewood, N.J.
Printed in U.S.A.

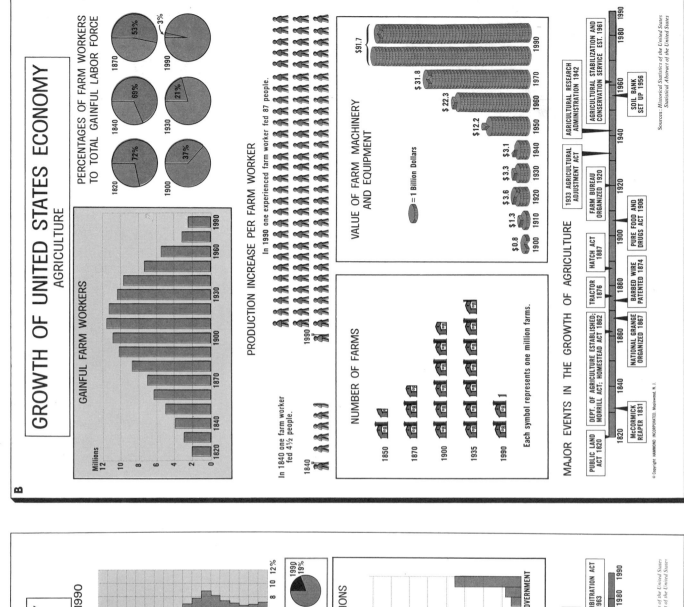

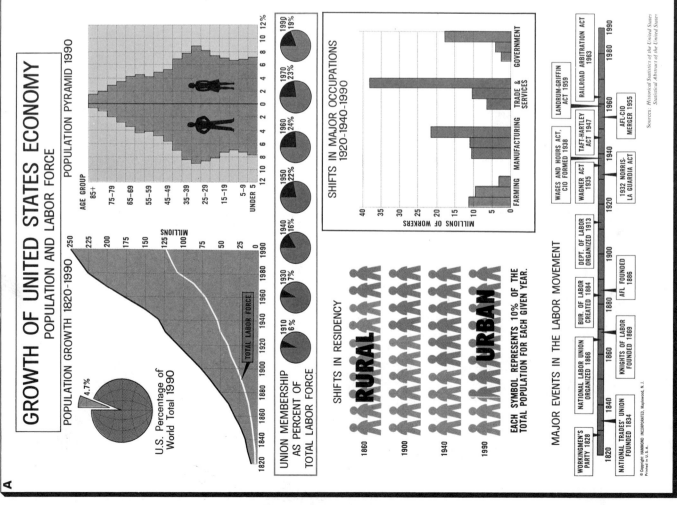

GROWTH OF UNITED STATES ECONOMY
NATIONAL PRODUCT AND INCOME

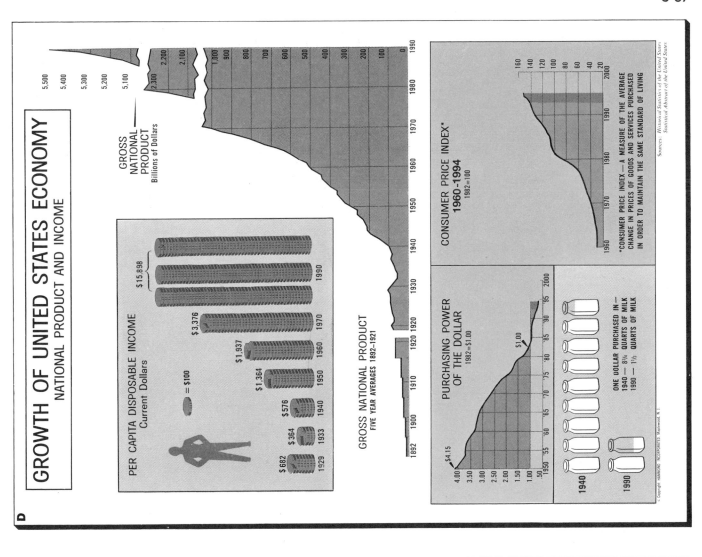

GROSS NATIONAL PRODUCT
Billions of Dollars

5,500 5,400 5,300 5,200 5,100 2,300 2,200 2,100 1,000 900 800 700 600 500 400 300 200 100 0

1990 1980 1970 1960 1950 1940 1930 1920 1910 1900

PER CAPITA DISPOSABLE INCOME
Current Dollars

= $100

$ 682 1929
$ 364 1933
$ 576 1940
$1,364 1950
$1,937 1960
$3,376 1970
$15,898 1990

GROSS NATIONAL PRODUCT
FIVE YEAR AVERAGES 1892–1921

1892 1900 1910 1920 1920

CONSUMER PRICE INDEX*
1960-1994
1982=100

160 140 120 100 80 60 40 20

2000 1990 1980 1970 1960

*CONSUMER PRICE INDEX – A MEASURE OF THE AVERAGE CHANGE IN PRICES OF GOODS AND SERVICES PURCHASED IN ORDER TO MAINTAIN THE SAME STANDARD OF LIVING

PURCHASING POWER OF THE DOLLAR
1982=$1.00

4.00 3.50 3.00 2.50 2.00 1.50 1.00 .50

$4.15

$1.00

1950 55 60 65 70 75 80 85 90 95 2000

ONE DOLLAR PURCHASED IN—
1940 — 8¾ QUARTS OF MILK
1990 — 1⅓ QUARTS OF MILK

1940
1990

Sources: *Historical Statistics of the United States*
Statistical Abstract of the United States

© Copyright HAMMOND INCORPORATED, Maplewood, N.J.

GROWTH OF UNITED STATES ECONOMY
TRANSPORTATION

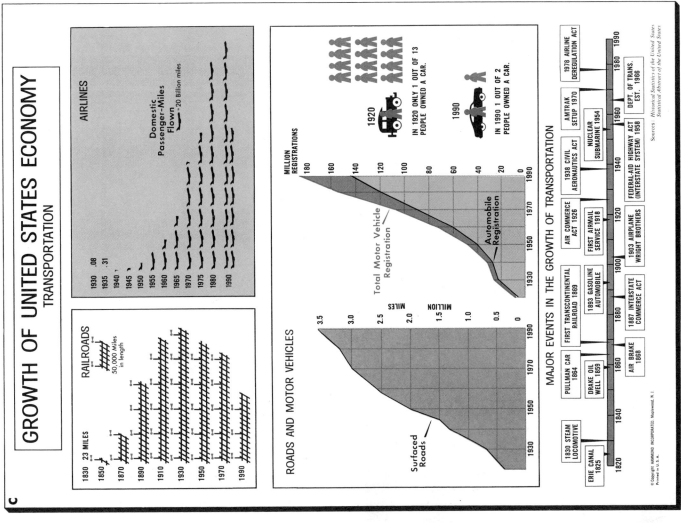

RAILROADS

= 50,000 Miles in length

1830 23 MILES
1850
1870
1890
1910
1930
1950
1970
1990

AIRLINES

Domestic Passenger-Miles Flown
= 20 Billion miles

1930 .08
1935 .31
1940
1945
1950
1955
1960
1965
1970
1975
1980
1990

ROADS AND MOTOR VEHICLES

MILLION REGISTRATIONS
180 160 140 120 100 80 60 40 20 0

Total Motor Vehicle Registration
Automobile Registration

1990 1970 1950 1930

MILES MILLION
3.5 3.0 2.5 2.0 1.5 1.0 0.5 0

Surfaced Roads

1930 1950 1970 1990

1920
IN 1920 ONLY 1 OUT OF 13 PEOPLE OWNED A CAR.

1990
IN 1990 1 OUT OF 2 PEOPLE OWNED A CAR.

MAJOR EVENTS IN THE GROWTH OF TRANSPORTATION

ERIE CANAL 1825
1830 STEAM LOCOMOTIVE
DRAKE OIL WELL 1859
AIR BRAKE 1868
PULLMAN CAR 1864
FIRST TRANSCONTINENTAL RAILROAD 1869
1887 INTERSTATE COMMERCE ACT
1893 GASOLINE AUTOMOBILE
1903 AIRPLANE WRIGHT BROTHERS
FIRST AIRMAIL SERVICE 1918
AIR COMMERCE ACT 1926
1938 CIVIL AERONAUTICS ACT
FEDERAL-AID HIGHWAY ACT (INTERSTATE SYSTEM) 1958
NUCLEAR SUBMARINE 1954
AMTRAK SETUP 1970
1978 AIRLINE DEREGULATION ACT
DEPT. OF TRANS. EST. 1966

1820 1840 1860 1880 1900 1920 1940 1960 1980 1990

Sources: *Historical Statistics of the United States*
Statistical Abstract of the United States

© Copyright HAMMOND INCORPORATED, Maplewood, N.J.
Printed in U.S.A.

C

D

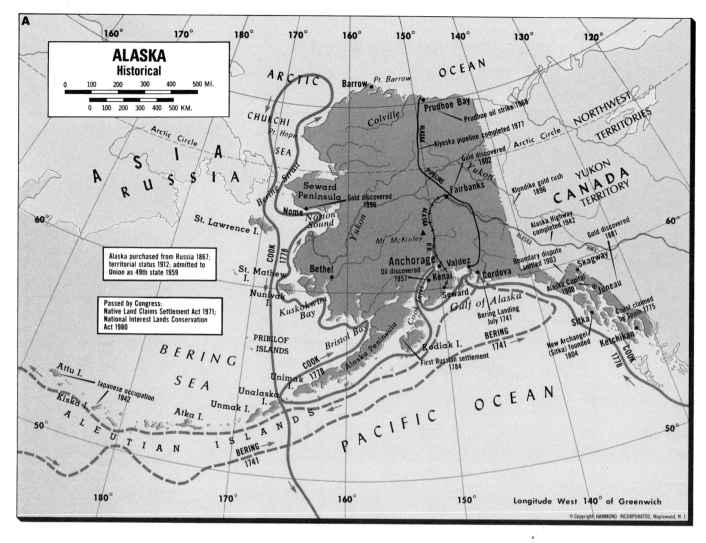

A

ALASKA
Historical

0 100 200 300 400 500 MI.

0 100 200 300 400 500 KM.

ARCTIC   OCEAN

Barrow   • Pt. Barrow

• Prudhoe Bay

Colville   Prudhoe oil strike 1968

CHUKCHI

Pt. Hope   Alyeska pipeline completed 1977   Arctic Circle   NORTHWEST

SEA   TERRITORIES

ASIA

RUSSIA   Gold discovered
1902

Seward   Yukon   Fairbanks   Klondike gold rush   YUKON
Peninsula   1896   CANADA

Gold discovered   TERRITORY
1899

Nome   Alaska Highway
Norton   Yukon   completed 1942   Gold discovered
Sound   1881

St. Lawrence I.   Mt. McKinley   Boundary dispute   Skagway
                                                        settled 1903

Alaska purchased from Russia 1867;   Anchorage   Alaska Capital
territorial status 1912; admitted to   Oil discovered   Valdez   1900   Juneau
Union as 49th state 1959   1957   Kenai   Cordova

St. Matthew   Seward   Sitka
I.   Gulf of Alaska

Passed by Congress: Bering Landing   New Archangel   Coast claimed
Native Land Claims Settlement Act 1971;   July 1741   (Sitka) founded   by Spain 1775
National Interest Lands Conservation   Nunivak   1804
Act 1980   I.   Ketchikan

Kuskokwim   Kodiak I.   BERING
Bay   1741

PRIBILOF   First Russian settlement
ISLANDS   Bristol Bay   1784

BERING   COOK   Alaska Peninsula
Unimak 1778

SEA   Unalaska   Unmak I.   PACIFIC   OCEAN
Attu I.   I.

Japanese occupation   Atka I.
1942

Kiska I.

ALEUTIAN   ISLANDS

BERING
1741

180°   170°   160°   150°   Longitude West 140° of Greenwich

© Copyright HAMMOND INCORPORATED, Maplewood, N.J.

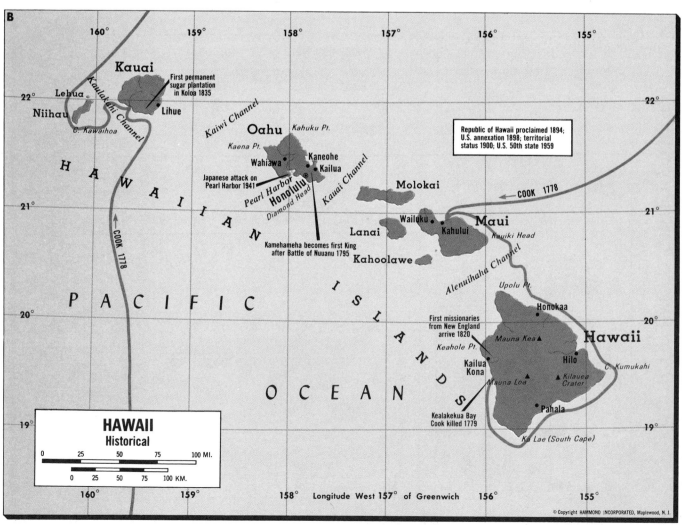

B

Kauai   First permanent
sugar plantation
in Koloa 1835

Lehua   Lihue

Niihau   Kaiwi Channel

C. Kawaihoa

Oahu   Kahuku Pt.

Kaena Pt.   Republic of Hawaii proclaimed 1894;
Wahiawa   Kaneohe   U.S. annexation 1898; territorial
Kailua   status 1900; U.S. 50th state 1959

Japanese attack on
Pearl Harbor 1941   Kauai Channel   Molokai   COOK 1778
Pearl Harbor   Honolulu
Diamond Head   Maui

HAWAIIAN   Lanai   Wailuku
Kamehameha becomes first King   Kahului   Kauiki Head
after Battle of Nuuanu 1795   Lanai

PACIFIC   Kahoolawe   Alenuihaha Channel

Upolu Pt.

First missionaries   Honokaa
from New England
arrive 1820   Mauna Kea ▲   Hawaii

ISLANDS   Keahole Pt.   Hilo

Kailua   C. Kumukahi
Kona   Kilauea
Mauna Loa ▲   Crater

HAWAII
Historical
0   25   50   75   100 MI.

0   25   50   75   100 KM.   Pahala

Kealakekua Bay
Cook killed 1779   Ka Lae (South Cape)

OCEAN

Longitude West 157° of Greenwich

© Copyright HAMMOND INCORPORATED, Maplewood, N.J.

THE FIFTY STATES

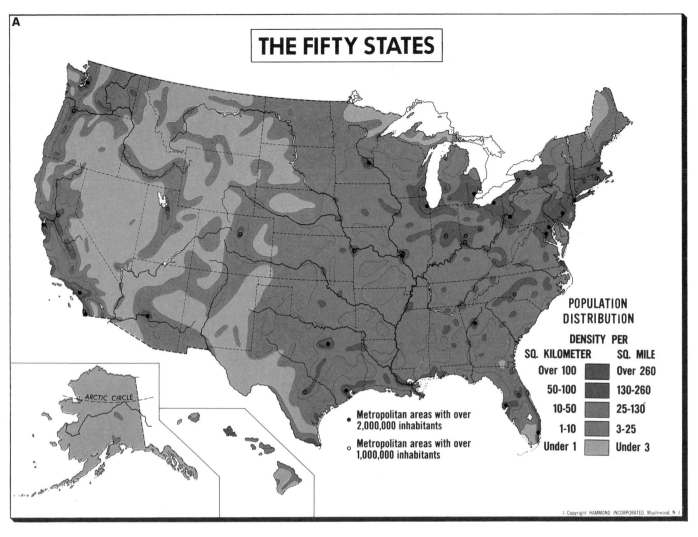

POPULATION DISTRIBUTION

DENSITY PER

SQ. KILOMETER		SQ. MILE
Over 100		Over 260
50-100		130-260
10-50		25-130
1-10		3-25
Under 1		Under 3

• Metropolitan areas with over 2,000,000 inhabitants

○ Metropolitan areas with over 1,000,000 inhabitants

ARCTIC CIRCLE

© Copyright HAMMOND INCORPORATED, Maplewood, N. J.

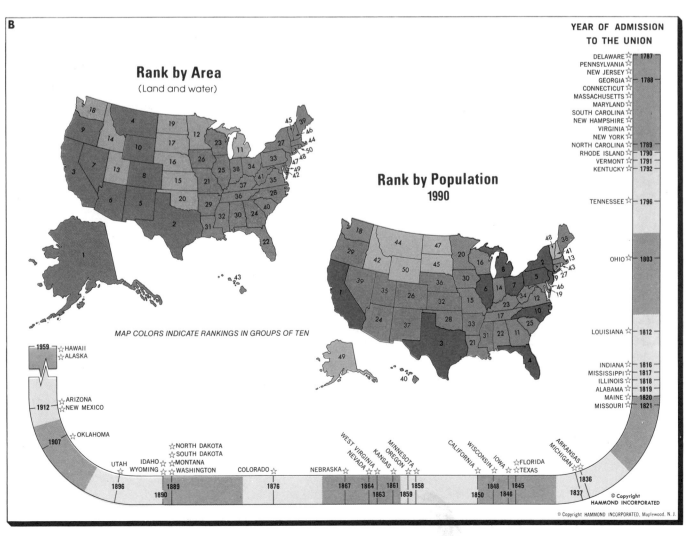

Rank by Area
(Land and water)

Rank by Population
1990

MAP COLORS INDICATE RANKINGS IN GROUPS OF TEN

YEAR OF ADMISSION TO THE UNION

DELAWARE ☆	1787
PENNSYLVANIA ☆	
NEW JERSEY ☆	
GEORGIA ☆	1788
CONNECTICUT ☆	
MASSACHUSETTS ☆	
MARYLAND ☆	
SOUTH CAROLINA ☆	
NEW HAMPSHIRE ☆	
VIRGINIA ☆	
NEW YORK ☆	
NORTH CAROLINA ☆	1789
RHODE ISLAND ☆	1790
VERMONT ☆	1791
KENTUCKY ☆	1792
TENNESSEE ☆	1796
OHIO ☆	1803
LOUISIANA ☆	1812
INDIANA ☆	1816
MISSISSIPPI ☆	1817
ILLINOIS ☆	1818
ALABAMA ☆	1819
MAINE ☆	1820
MISSOURI ☆	1821

1959 ☆ HAWAII
☆ ALASKA

1912 ☆ ARIZONA
☆ NEW MEXICO

1907 ☆ OKLAHOMA

☆ NORTH DAKOTA
☆ SOUTH DAKOTA
UTAH ☆ IDAHO ☆ ☆ MONTANA
WYOMING ☆ ☆ WASHINGTON
COLORADO ☆
☆ WEST VIRGINIA
NEBRASKA ☆ ☆ NEVADA
KANSAS
OREGON
☆ MINNESOTA
CALIFORNIA ☆
☆ WISCONSIN
☆ IOWA
☆ FLORIDA
☆ TEXAS
ARKANSAS
MICHIGAN

1896   1889   1867   1864   1861   1858   1848   1845   1836
   1890   1876   1863   1859   1850   1846   1837

© Copyright HAMMOND INCORPORATED

© Copyright HAMMOND INCORPORATED, Maplewood, N. J.

POPULATION CHARACTERISTICS

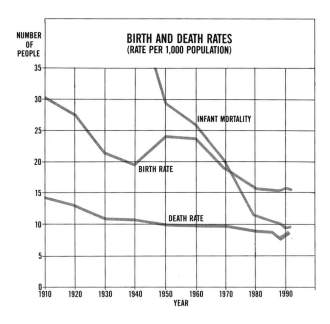

BIRTH AND DEATH RATES
(RATE PER 1,000 POPULATION)

NUMBER OF PEOPLE

INFANT MORTALITY

BIRTH RATE

DEATH RATE

YEAR

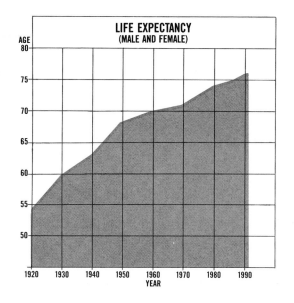

LIFE EXPECTANCY
(MALE AND FEMALE)

AGE

YEAR

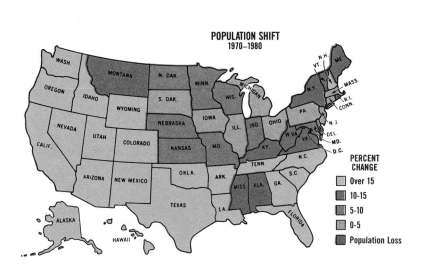

POPULATION SHIFT
1970–1980

PERCENT CHANGE

Over 15
10-15
5-10
0-5
Population Loss

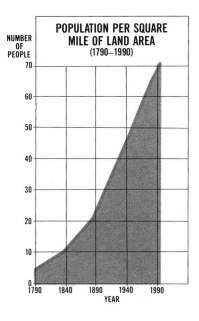

POPULATION PER SQUARE MILE OF LAND AREA
(1790–1990)

NUMBER OF PEOPLE

YEAR

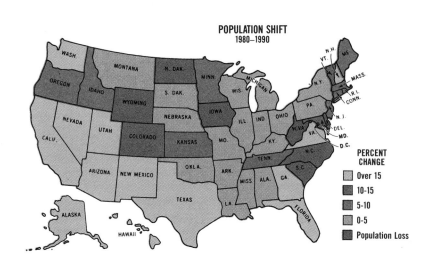

POPULATION SHIFT
1980–1990

PERCENT CHANGE

Over 15
10-15
5-10
0-5
Population Loss

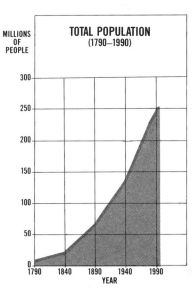

TOTAL POPULATION
(1790–1990)

MILLIONS OF PEOPLE

YEAR

Source: *Statistical Abstract of the United States*

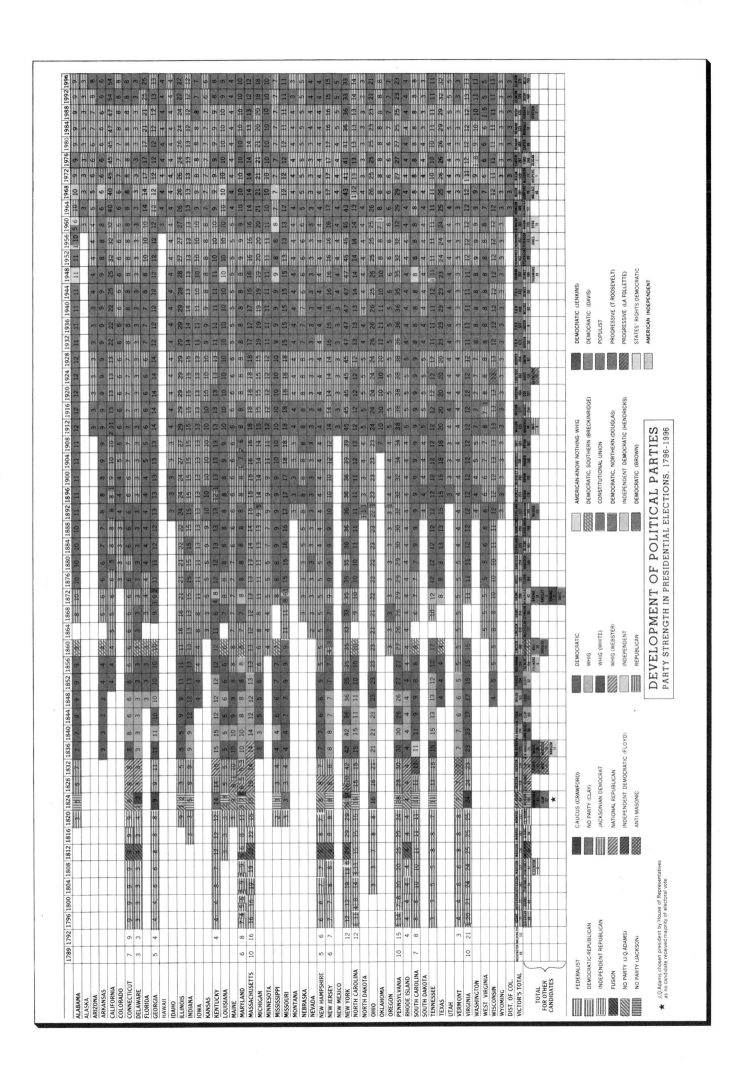

DEVELOPMENT OF POLITICAL PARTIES
PARTY STRENGTH IN PRESIDENTIAL ELECTIONS, 1796-1996

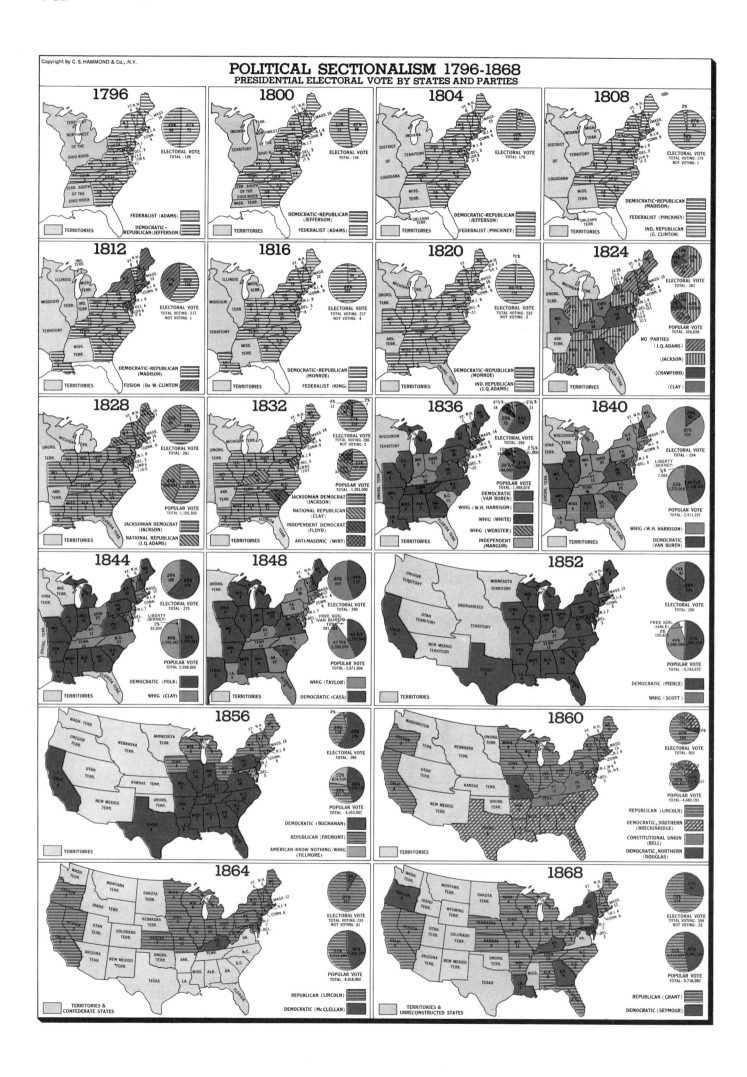

Copyright by C.S. HAMMOND & Co., .N.Y.

POLITICAL SECTIONALISM 1796-1868
PRESIDENTIAL ELECTORAL VOTE BY STATES AND PARTIES

POLITICAL SECTIONALISM 1872-1916
PRESIDENTIAL ELECTORAL VOTE BY STATES AND PARTIES

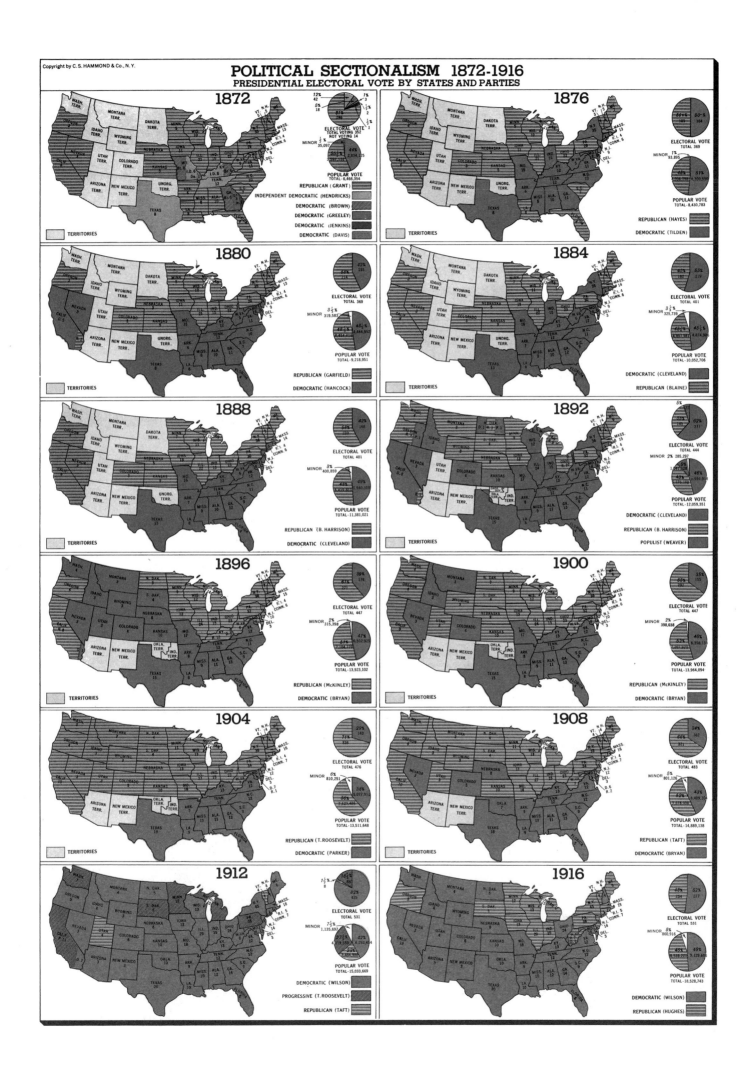

1872

ELECTORAL VOTE
TOTAL VOTING 352
NOT VOTING 14

MINOR ½%
35,097

POPULAR VOTE
TOTAL - 6,466,354

REPUBLICAN (GRANT)
INDEPENDENT DEMOCRATIC (HENDRICKS)
DEMOCRATIC (BROWN)
DEMOCRATIC (GREELEY)
DEMOCRATIC (JENKINS)
DEMOCRATIC (DAVIS)

TERRITORIES

1876

ELECTORAL VOTE
TOTAL 369

MINOR 1%
93,895

POPULAR VOTE
TOTAL - 8,430,783

REPUBLICAN (HAYES)
DEMOCRATIC (TILDEN)

TERRITORIES

1880

ELECTORAL VOTE
TOTAL 369

MINOR 319,585

POPULAR VOTE
TOTAL - 9,218,951

REPUBLICAN (GARFIELD)
DEMOCRATIC (HANCOCK)

TERRITORIES

1884

ELECTORAL VOTE
TOTAL 401

MINOR 3½%
325,739

POPULAR VOTE
TOTAL - 10,052,706

DEMOCRATIC (CLEVELAND)
REPUBLICAN (BLAINE)

TERRITORIES

1888

ELECTORAL VOTE
TOTAL 401

MINOR 3%
400,859

POPULAR VOTE
TOTAL - 11,381,021

REPUBLICAN (B. HARRISON)
DEMOCRATIC (CLEVELAND)

TERRITORIES

1892

ELECTORAL VOTE
TOTAL 444

MINOR 2% 285,297

POPULAR VOTE
TOTAL - 12,059,351

DEMOCRATIC (CLEVELAND)
REPUBLICAN (B. HARRISON)
POPULIST (WEAVER)

TERRITORIES

1896

ELECTORAL VOTE
TOTAL 447

MINOR 2%
315,398

POPULAR VOTE
TOTAL - 13,923,102

REPUBLICAN (McKINLEY)
DEMOCRATIC (BRYAN)

TERRITORIES

1900

ELECTORAL VOTE
TOTAL 447

MINOR 2%
398,038

POPULAR VOTE
TOTAL - 13,964,094

REPUBLICAN (McKINLEY)
DEMOCRATIC (BRYAN)

TERRITORIES

1904

ELECTORAL VOTE
TOTAL 476

MINOR 6%
810,251

POPULAR VOTE
TOTAL - 13,511,648

REPUBLICAN (T. ROOSEVELT)
DEMOCRATIC (PARKER)

TERRITORIES

1908

ELECTORAL VOTE
TOTAL 483

MINOR 5%
801,126

POPULAR VOTE
TOTAL - 14,889,138

REPUBLICAN (TAFT)
DEMOCRATIC (BRYAN)

TERRITORIES

1912

ELECTORAL VOTE
TOTAL 531

MINOR 7½%
1,135,697

POPULAR VOTE
TOTAL - 15,033,669

DEMOCRATIC (WILSON)
PROGRESSIVE (T. ROOSEVELT)
REPUBLICAN (TAFT)

1916

ELECTORAL VOTE
TOTAL 531

MINOR 5%
860,916

POPULAR VOTE
TOTAL - 18,528,743

DEMOCRATIC (WILSON)
REPUBLICAN (HUGHES)

POLITICAL SECTIONALISM 1920-1964
PRESIDENTIAL ELECTORAL VOTE BY STATES AND PARTIES

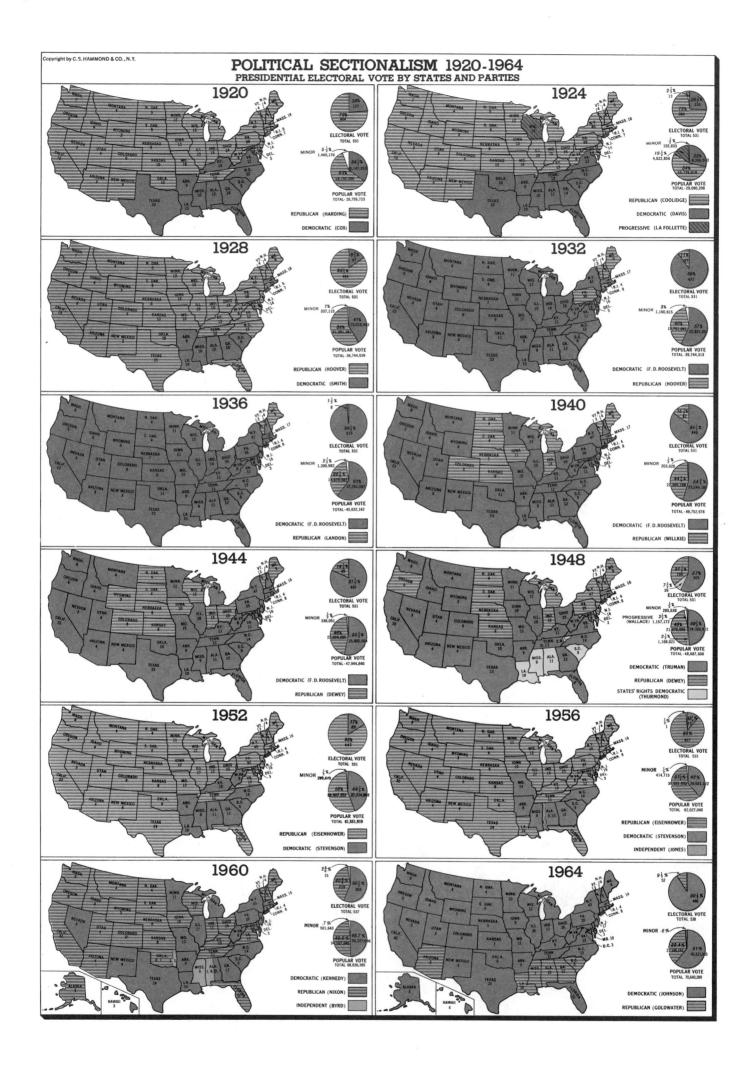

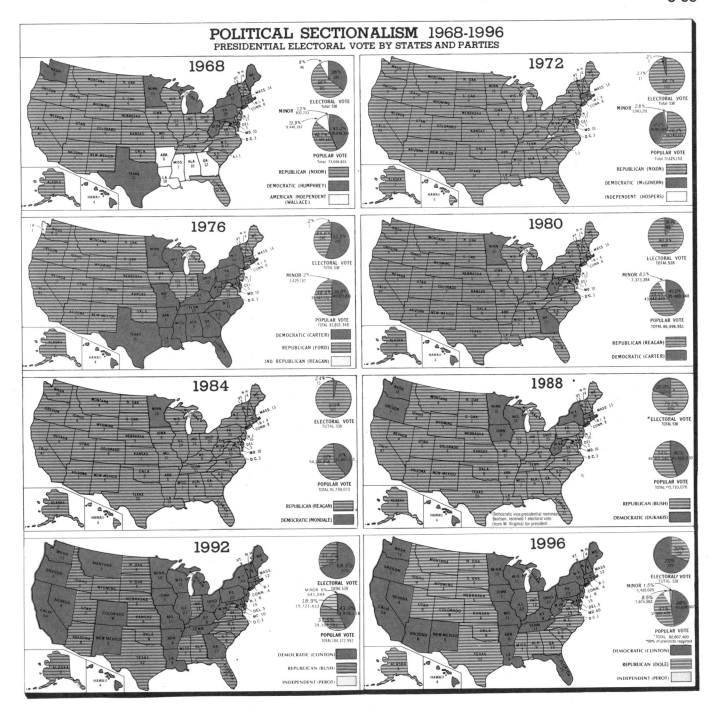

PRESIDENTS OF THE UNITED STATES

No.	Name	Politics	Native State	Age at Inaugu- ration	Age at Death	No.	Name	Politics	Native State	Age at Inaugu- ration	Age at Death
1	George Washington	Federalist	Va.	57	67	22	Grover Cleveland	Democrat	N.J.	47	71
2	John Adams	Federalist	Mass.	61	90	23	Benjamin Harrison	Republican	Ohio	55	67
3	Thomas Jefferson	Rep.-Dem.	Va.	57	83	24	Grover Cleveland	Democrat	N.J.	55	71
4	James Madison	Rep.-Dem.	Va.	57	85	25	William McKinley	Republican	Ohio	54	58
5	James Monroe	Rep.-Dem.	Va.	58	73	26	Theodore Roosevelt	Republican	N.Y.	42	60
6	John Quincy Adams	Rep.-Dem.	Mass.	57	80	27	William Howard Taft	Republican	Ohio	51	72
7	Andrew Jackson	Democrat	S.C.	61	78	28	Woodrow Wilson	Democrat	Va.	56	67
8	Martin Van Buren	Democrat	N.Y.	54	79	29	Warren G. Harding	Republican	Ohio	55	57
9	William Henry Harrison	Whig	Va.	68	68	30	Calvin Coolidge	Republican	Vt.	51	60
10	John Tyler	Whig	Va.	51	71	31	Herbert Clark Hoover	Republican	Iowa	54	90
11	James Knox Polk	Democrat	N.C.	49	53	32	Franklin D. Roosevelt	Democrat	N.Y.	51	63
12	Zachary Taylor	Whig	Va.	64	65	33	Harry S Truman	Democrat	Mo.	60	88
13	Millard Fillmore	Whig	N.Y.	50	74	34	Dwight D. Eisenhower	Republican	Texas	62	78
14	Franklin Pierce	Democrat	N.H.	48	64	35	John F. Kennedy	Democrat	Mass.	43	46
15	James Buchanan	Democrat	Pa.	65	77	36	Lyndon B. Johnson	Democrat	Texas	55	64
16	Abraham Lincoln	Republican	Ky.	52	56	37	Richard M. Nixon	Republican	Calif.	56	81
17	Andrew Johnson	Democrat	N.C.	56	66	38	Gerald R. Ford	Republican	Mich.	61	—
18	Ulysses Simpson Grant	Republican	Ohio	46	63	39	James E. Carter, Jr.	Democrat	Ga.	52	—
19	Rutherford B. Hayes	Republican	Ohio	54	70	40	Ronald W. Reagan	Republican	Ill.	69	—
20	James Abram Garfield	Republican	Ohio	49	49	41	George H. W. Bush	Republican	Mass.	64	—
21	Chester Alan Arthur	Republican	Vt.	50	56	42	William J. Clinton	Democrat	Ark.	46	—

Flags of American History

FLAGS OF DISCOVERY AND SETTLEMENT

FLAG OF LEIF ERICKSON—1000
RAVEN OF THE VIKINGS, FIRST FLAG CARRIED
TO AMERICA'S SHORES.

**EXPEDITIONARY FLAG OF COLUMBUS
1492**

FLAG OF COLUMBUS 1492—1498
STANDARD OF FERDINAND AND ISABELLA.
RAISED AT SAN SALVADOR 1492, MAINLAND, 1498.

FLAG OF JOHN CABOT—1497
CROSS OF ST. GEORGE. FIRST FLAG RAISED
ON MAINLAND. RALEIGH'S FLAG 1585.

FLAG OF CHAMPLAIN—1603
BORNE BY CARTIER, JOLIET, MARQUETTE, LA SALLE
AND OTHER INTREPID FRENCH VOYAGEURS.

FLAG OF HUDSON—1607
FIRST FLAG RAISED AT NEW YORK, VERRAZANO DIS-
COVERED THE RIVER EIGHTY FOUR YEARS EARLIER.

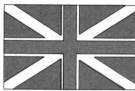

FLAG OF THE MAYFLOWER—1620
FLAG BORNE ON THE MAIN MAST OF THE MAYFLOWER
BY THE PILGRIM FATHERS.

FLAG OF SWEDEN—1638
ENSIGN OF NEW SWEDEN RAISED ON THE
DELAWARE RIVER.

FLAGS OF COLONIAL DAYS

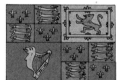

STUART STANDARD 1603—1649, 1660—1689

CROMWELL'S STANDARD 1653—1660

ROYAL STANDARD 1689—1702

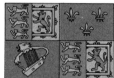

ROYAL STANDARD 1707—1714

ROYAL STANDARD 1714—1801

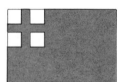

ENGLISH RED ENSIGN
THE FAMOUS METEOR FLAG OF OLD ENGLAND
AND ENSIGN OF COLONIES 17TH CENTURY.

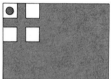

ENDICOTT FLAG—1634
THE SALEM ENSIGN SHOWING RELIGIOUS
OPPOSITION TO CROSS IN CANTON.

THREE COUNTY TROUP—1659
FLAG OF THE THREE MASSACHUSETTS COUNTIES
AND EMBLEM OF KING PHILIP'S WAR, 1675—1676.

ESCUTCHEONED JACK—1701
FLAG DESIGNED FOR MERCHANT SHIPS
OF HIS MAJESTY'S PLANTATIONS.

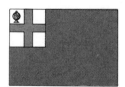

NEW ENGLAND FLAG—1737
THIS ENSIGN SHOWS THE EARLY TENDENCY
OF THE COLONIES TO FIND INDIVIDUAL FLAGS.

FLAGS OF THE REVOLUTION

TAUNTON FLAG—1774
ONE OF THE EARLIEST EMBLEMS
OF THE REVOLUTION.

BEDFORD FLAG—1775
CARRIED BY REVERE AND DAWES
IN AROUSING THE MINUTE MEN.

CULPEPER FLAG—1775
ONE OF THE EARLY RATTLESNAKE FLAGS
CARRIED BY THE MINUTE MEN.

PHILADELPHIA LIGHT HORSE
WASHINGTON'S ESCORT TO COMMAND
OF THE CONTINENTAL ARMY, 1775.

RHODE ISLAND FLAG—1776
CARRIED AT BRANDYWINE, TRENTON AND
YORKTOWN.

FORT MOULTRIE FLAG—1776
NAILED TO STAFF BY SERGEANT JASPER
WHEN SHOT AWAY.

LIBERTY TREE FLAG—1776
THE PINE TREE COMES FROM COINS OF THE
COLONY OF MASSACHUSETTS, 1652.

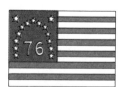

BENNINGTON FLAG—1777
FLAG OF VICTORY OF THE GREEN MOUNTAIN
BOYS.

BENJAMIN FRANKLIN FLAG
ALSO CALLED "SERAPIS" FLAG. GENERALLY ACCEPTED AS
ORIGINATED BY BENJAMIN FRANKLIN AT COURT OF LOUIS XVI.

MERCHANT ENSIGN 1776—1795
AN EMBLEM IN GENERAL USE, ALSO
PRIVATEER'S FLAG.

FLAGS OF THE OLD NAVY

GADSDEN FLAG—1775
COMMODORE ESEK HOPKINS' ENSIGN USED IN HIS FIRST
FLEET COMMAND.

WASHINGTON'S NAVY ENSIGN—1775
THE FLAG OF THE SIX CRUISERS THAT FORMED THE FIRST
AMERICAN NAVAL FLEET.

FIRST NAVY JACK—1775
HOSTED AT THE MAIN MAST BY COMMANDER-IN-CHIEF ESEK HOPKINS,
DECEMBER 3, 1775.

FLAGS OF THE YOUNG REPUBLIC

FIRST NAVY STARS AND STRIPES
IN ABSENCE OF SPECIFIC ARRANGEMENT OF STARS BY CONGRESS JUNE 14, 1777
IT WAS CUSTOMARY FOR NAVY TO PLACE THE STARS IN FORM OF CROSSES OF
ST. GEORGE AND ST. ANDREW.

"STAR SPANGLED BANNER"—1814
THE EMBLEM OF INSPIRATION OF OUR NATIONAL ANTHEM, 1814.
FLAG OF VICTORY OVER BARBARY PIRATES 1803 TO 1805.

FREMONT THE PATHFINDER'S FLAG—40'S
EMBLEM THAT BLAZED THE TRAIL FOR THE COVERED WAGON
IN THE ROARING 40'S. THE EARLY ENSIGN OF THE PLAINS.

FAMOUS BATTLE FLAGS

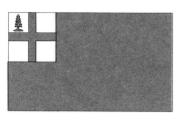

BUNKER HILL FLAG—1775
HISTORIC EMBLEM THAT PROVED THE STRENGTH OF THE SPIRIT
OF AMERICAN LIBERTY. CARRIED AT LEXINGTON AND CONCORD.

CAMBRIDGE FLAG, FIRST NAVY ENSIGN 1775–1776
HOISTED BY JOHN PAUL JONES, DECEMBER 3, 1775 AND BY
GENERAL WASHINGTON, JANUARY 2, 1776.

CONTINENTAL FLAG
CARRIED IN 1775–1777, SHOWING PINE TREE, SYMBOL OF
MASSACHUSETTS BAY COLONY, IN PLACE OF THE CROSSES OF
ST. GEORGE AND ST. ANDREW.

FLAGS OF THE CONFEDERACY

FIRST CONFEDERATE FLAG
FAMOUS "STARS AND BARS" USED FROM MARCH 1861 TO MAY 1863.

SECOND CONFEDERATE FLAG
NATIONAL EMBLEM FROM MAY 1, 1863 TO MARCH 4, 1865.

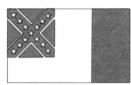

THIRD CONFEDERATE FLAG
NATIONAL EMBLEM ADOPTED MARCH 8, 1865.

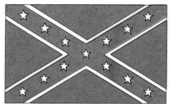

CONFEDERATE NAVY FLAG
USED FROM MAY 1, 1863 TO END OF WAR, 1865.
THE BATTLE FLAG WAS SQUARE.

OTHER NOTEWORTHY FLAGS OF AMERICAN HISTORY

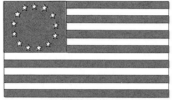

FIRST STARS AND STRIPES
UNITED EMBLEM OF INDEPENDENCE SAID TO HAVE ORIGINATED BY
GEORGE WASHINGTON FOLLOWING ACT OF CONGRESS OF JUNE 14, 1777.

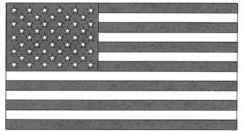

PRESENT DAY FLAG

"OLD GLORY"
NAME GIVEN BY CAPTAIN WILLIAM DRIVER, COMMANDING THE BRIG
"CHARLES DAGGETT" IN 1831.

FLAG OF THE THIRD MARYLAND REGIMENT—1778
CARRIED AT THE BATTLE OF COWPENS JANUARY, 1778 AND USED AS COLORS OF
AMERICAN LAND FORCES UNTIL MEXICAN WAR.

NAPOLEON'S LOUISIANA FLAG
THIS FLAG WAS REPLACED BY "STARS AND STRIPES"
FOLLOWING LOUISIANA PURCHASE DECEMBER 24, 1803.

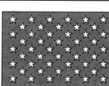

U.S. NAVY JACK
USED BY NAVAL VESSELS AND
MARITIME GOVERNORS.

FLAG OF THE MEXICAN WAR—1845
NOT ACTUALLY USED AS REGIMENTAL COLORS BY TROOPS, BUT AS FLAG
OF CONQUEST AND OCCUPATION.

FLAG OF THE WAR OF 1812 (1812–1814)
SHOWING FIFTEEN STARS AND FIFTEEN BARS AS CHANGED UPON
ADMISSION OF VERMONT.

RUSSIAN AMERICAN CO'S. FLAG
EMBLEM RAISED 1799, REPLACED BY
"STARS AND STRIPES" 1867.

U.S. COAST GUARD FLAG
WITHOUT EMBLEM ON FLY THIS IS
U.S. CUSTOMS FLAG.

FLAG OF THE CIVIL WAR 1861–1865
THE "STARS AND STRIPES" WITH THIRTY SIX STARS IN THE UNION CARRIED
BY THE NORTHERN ARMIES DURING LATER YEARS OF THE CIVIL WAR.

THE FLAG OF 1818
SHOWING RETURN TO THIRTEEN STRIPES AND ADDITIONAL STARS IN CANTON.

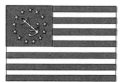

COMMODORE PERRY'S FLAG—1854
THE FLAG THAT OPENED JAPAN
TO WESTERN CIVILIZATION.

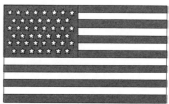

AMERICAN YACHT ENSIGN
AUTHORIZED BY ACT OF CONGRESS
AUGUST 7, 1848.

FLAG OF THE SPANISH-AMERICAN WAR—1898
THE EMBLEM OF LIBERTY THAT BROUGHT FREEDOM TO CUBA.

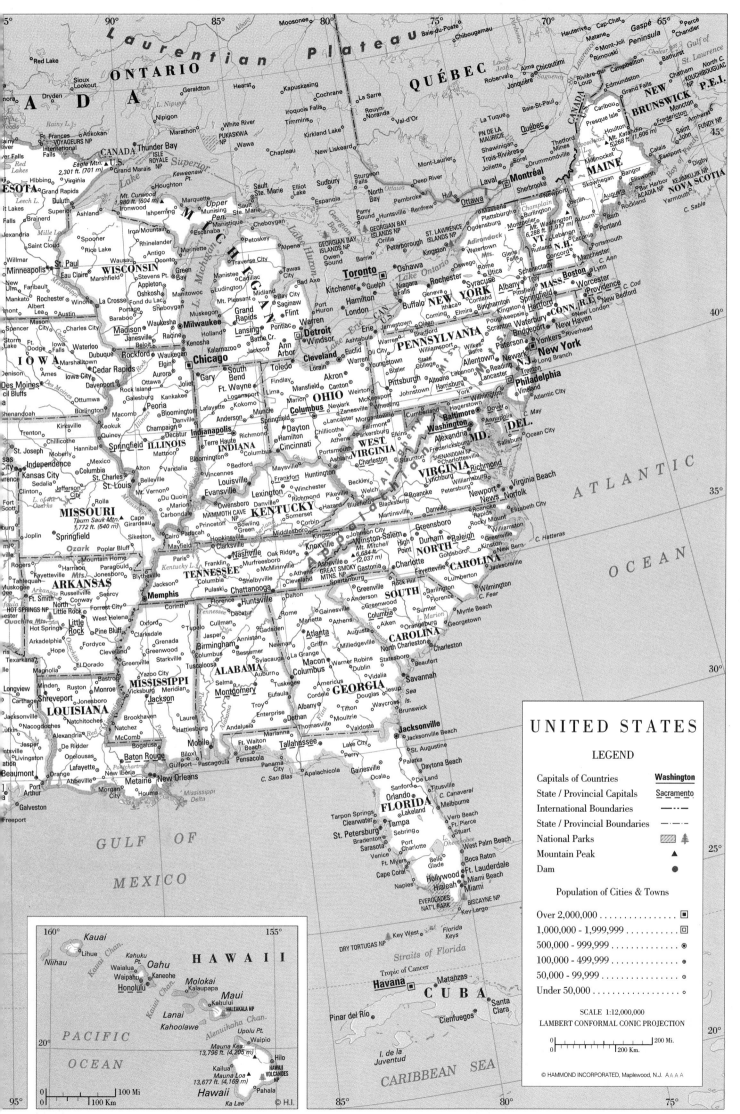

UNITED STATES

LEGEND

Capitals of Countries	**Washington**
State / Provincial Capitals	Sacramento
International Boundaries	— ·· — ·· —
State / Provincial Boundaries	— · — · —
National Parks	▨ ♠
Mountain Peak	▲
Dam	●

Population of Cities & Towns

Over 2,000,000	▣
1,000,000 - 1,999,999	▢
500,000 - 999,999	◉
100,000 - 499,999	⊛
50,000 - 99,999	⊚
Under 50,000	○

SCALE 1:12,000,000
LAMBERT CONFORMAL CONIC PROJECTION

0 ———— 200 Mi.
0 ———— 200 Km.

© HAMMOND INCORPORATED, Maplewood, N.J. A A A A

Flags of States, Territories and Possessions

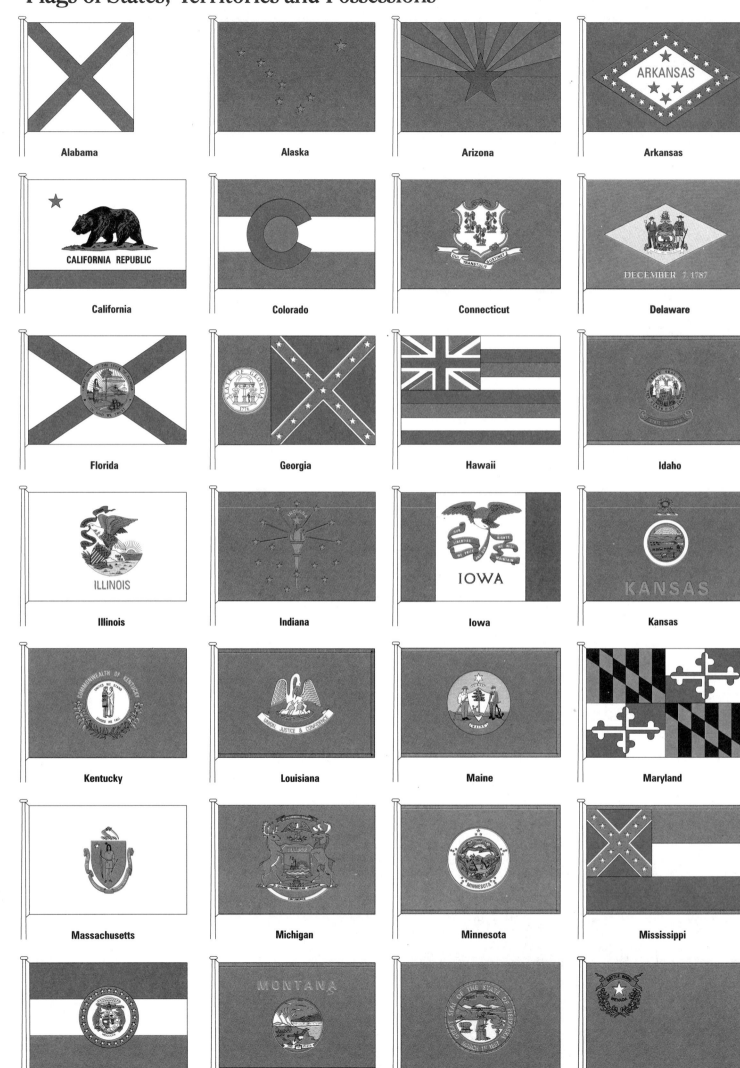

Alabama	Alaska	Arizona	Arkansas
California	Colorado	Connecticut	Delaware
Florida	Georgia	Hawaii	Idaho
Illinois	Indiana	Iowa	Kansas
Kentucky	Louisiana	Maine	Maryland
Massachusetts	Michigan	Minnesota	Mississippi
Missouri	Montana	Nebraska	Nevada

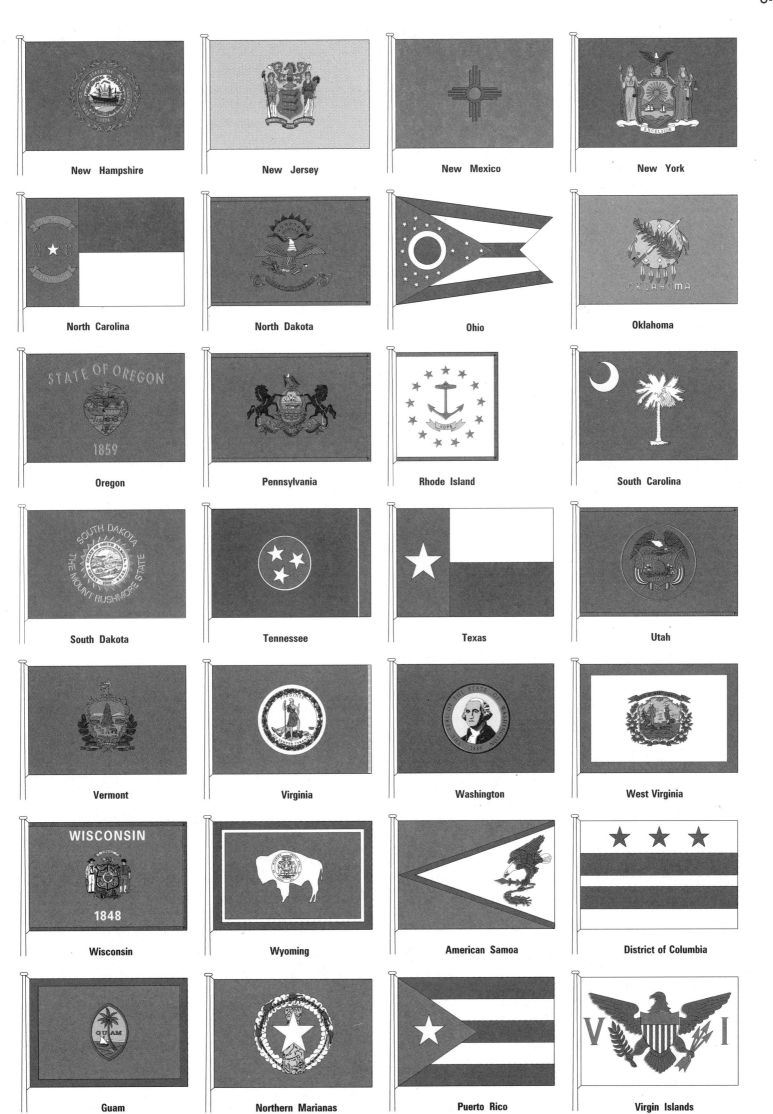

New Hampshire

New Jersey

New Mexico

New York

North Carolina

North Dakota

Ohio

Oklahoma

Oregon

Pennsylvania

Rhode Island

South Carolina

South Dakota

Tennessee

Texas

Utah

Vermont

Virginia

Washington

West Virginia

Wisconsin

Wyoming

American Samoa

District of Columbia

Guam

Northern Marianas

Puerto Rico

Virgin Islands

Index

This index lists historically important places, areas, events and geographical features appearing on the maps of the United States History Atlas. Each entry is followed by the page number on which the name appears. The letters following the page number designate a particular map on pages containing more than one map. Names that appear on more than one map are indexed to the map or maps portraying the place at its most historically significant period.

Abilene, Kansas ..30A, 30B, 30C
Acadia 7B, 10A, 10B, 11C
Alamo, the 21A
Alaska 16B, 58A
Albany, N. Y. 9C, 11C, 12A, 14B, 20A, 20B
Antietam, Battle of 24A, 26A
Appalachian Mountains 6B
Appomattox Court House 25C, 27C
Argonne Forest 41C
Arkansas Territory 22A
Armistice Line 40B
Army Posts in the West........31D
Atlanta, Ga. 25C
Augusta, Ga. 15C
Ballistic Missile Early Warning System (BMEWS) 51D
Baltimore, Md. 12A, 26B
Belleau Wood 41C
Bennington, Battle of 14B
Bent's Fort 20A, 21B
Bladensburg, Battle of.........19C
Bloody Marsh, Battle of.........10B
Boston, Mass. 12A, 14A, 15D
Brandy Station, Battle of 26B
Brandywine, Battle of 14B
Breeds Hill 15D
Buena Vista, Battle of 21B
Bulge, Battle of the 47D
Bull Run, Battle of 24A, 25C, 26A
Bunker Hill, Battle of..14A, 15D
Butterfield Overland Mail 20A
Cahokia, Ill. 11D, 15D
California 13D, 30A
California Trail 20A
Camden, S. C. 12A, 12B, 13C, 15C
Canal Zone 32B
Carolina 9D
Cedar Creek, Battle of 27C
Cedar Mountain, Battle of....26A
Central Pacific Railroad.......30A
Cerro Gordo, Battle of 21B
Champlain, Lake 6B, 11C, 14A, 14B, 18A, 18B, 19C
Chancellorsville, Battle of....26B
Chantilly, Battle of 26A
Château Thierry 40B, 41C
Chapultepec 21B
Charleston, S.C. 12A, 14A, 14B, 15C, 24A
Chateaugay, Battle of 18B
Chattanooga, Battle of 24B
Chesapeake and Ohio Canal..20B
Chicago Pike 20A
Chickamauga, Battle of 24B
Chippewa, Battle of 19C
Chisholm Trail 30A
Chrysler's Farm, Battle of 18B
Churubusco, Battle of 21B
Cibola 6B
Cold Harbor, Battle of 27C
Coleto, Battle of 21A
Colorado Territory 23D
Columbia River 6B
Comstock Lode ..30A, 30B, 31C
Concepción, Battle of 21A
Concord, Battle of 15D
Connecticut 12A, 17
Connecticut Colony 9D
Contreras, Battle of 21B
Coral Sea, Battle of 48B
Council Bluffs, Iowa 20A
Council Grove, Kansas 20A
Cowpens, Battle of 15C
Creek War 18B, 19C
Cripple Creek, Colorado 31C
Cross Keys, Battle of 26A
Cuba 5A, 7B, 7C, 7D, 32A, 33C
Cumberland Gap 20A
Dakota Territory 23D
Defiance, Fort 18A, 18B
Delaware 9D, 17
Detroit, Fort 11D
Detroit, Mich. 17, 18B
Distant Early Warning Line (DEW) 51D
Dodge City, Kansas 30B
Dominican Republic 32B, 33C
Dorchester Heights 15D
Dred Scott Decision 23D
Dunkirk, France 46B
Duquesne, Fort ...10B, 11C, 11D
Dust Bowl 45C
El Caney, Battle of 32A
El Paso, Texas 21B
Erie, Lake 6B
Erie Canal 20B
Fisher's Hill, Battle of 27C
Five Forks, Battle of 27C
Florida 7B, 7C, 7D, 16B
Florida, East 16B
Florida, West 16B
Fort Donelson, Battle of 24A
Fort Morgan, Battle of 25C
Fort Pulaski, Battle of 24A
Fredericksburg, Battle of 26A, 26B
Front Royal, Battle of 26A
Gadsden Purchase 16B, 23C
Genesee Road 20A
Georgia 9D, 17
Germantown, Battle of 14B
Gettysburg, Battle of...........24B, 26B, 27D
Godly Wood, Battle of 19C
Goliad, Texas 21A
Goodnight Loving Trail........30A
Great Basin 6B
Great Plains 6B
Guadalcanal, Battle of 49C
Guadalupe Hidalgo, Treaty of 21B
Guilford Court House, Battle of 15C
Haiti 32B
Halifax, Nova Scotia 11C
Harpers Ferry, W. Va. 20A, 26A
Harrodsburg, Ky. 20A
Hartford, Conn. 9D
Havana, Cuba 32A, 32B, 33C
Hawaii 16B,58B
Hiroshima, Japan 49C
Hispaniola 5A
Honduras 32B
Horseshoe Bend, Battle of....19C
Hudson's Bay Company 7B, 7C, 7D
Hudson River 6B, 14B
Independence, Mo. 20A
Indiana Territory 18A, 18B, 19C
Indian archaeological sites 4B
Indian culture areas 4B
Indian raids 10A, 10B, 11C, 15D, 30A, 30B, 31C
Indian reservations 31D
Indian Territory ..23D, 31C, 31D
Indians, major tribes of 4A
Indians, linguistic families of...4A
Iroquois Indians ..10A, 10B, 11C
Iwo Jima, Battle of 49C
Jackson Military Road 20A
Jamestown, Va. 6B, 8A, 8B
Jenkins' Ear, War of 10B
Kansas-Nebraska Act 23C
Kansas Territory 23C
Kaskaskia, Ill. 11D, 15D
Kearney, Fort 20A
Kernstown, Battle of 26A
King George's War 10B
Kings Mountain, Battle of 15C
King William's War 10A
Korea 53C
La Guasimas, Battle of 32A
Lake Erie, Battle of 18B
Lead, S. Dak. 30B
Lexington, Battle of 15D
Little Bighorn, Battle of........30B
London Company 8A
Long Island 7A, 9D, 14A
Los Angeles, Calif. 13D, 21B
Louisbourg, Fortress of 10B, 11C
Louisiana 7B, 7C, 7D
Louisiana Purchase 16B
Lundy's Lane, Battle of........19C
McHenry, Fort 19C
Magellan, Strait of 5B
Maine 9C, 10A, 10B, 11C, 17
Marianas, Battle of 49C
Maryland 9C
Mason-Dixon Line 23D
Massachusetts 17
Massachusetts Bay Company..9C
Maysville Road 20A
Meigs, Fort 18B
Mexican Cession 16B
Miami, Fort 17
Michigan Road 20A
Michigan Territory 18A, 18B, 19C
Michilimackinac, Fort ..11D, 17
Midway, Battle of 48B
Minnesota Territory 22B
Mississippi River 6B
Mississippi Territory 18A, 18B, 19C
Missouri Compromise 23C
Missouri River 6B
Mobile, Ala. 11D, 25C
Mohawk River 10A, 10B, 11C, 14B
Molina del Rey, Battle of......21B
Monocacy, Battle of 27C
Monmouth Court House, Battle of 14B
Monterrey, Battle of 21B
Montreal, Canada 6B, 10A, 11C, 11D, 14A, 14B, 18A
Mormon Settlement 20A
Mormon Trail 20A
Morristown, New Jersey 14A, 14B, 15C
Nashville, Tennessee ...20A, 25C
Natchez, Miss. 11D, 20A
Natchez Trace 20A
National Pike 20A
Nebraska Territory 23C, 23D
Necessity, Fort 10B
Nevada Territory 23D
New Albion 6B
New Amsterdam (New York) 9C
New Bern, N.C. 12A, 24A
New Castle, Del. 12A, 12B, 13C
New England 7B, 7C, 7D
Newfoundland 5A, 7A, 7B, 7C, 7D
New France 5A, 7B, 7C, 10A, 10B, 11C, 11D
New Granada 7B, 7C, 7D
New Hampshire 9C, 10A, 10B, 11C, 17
New Haven, Conn. 9D
New Haven Colony 9D
New Jersey 9D
New Mexico 11D
New Mexico Territory 22B, 23C, 23D
New Netherlands 9C
New Orleans, La. 11D, 19C, 24A, 25C
Newport, R. I. 12A, 15C
New Spain 5A, 7B, 7C, 7D, 11D
New Sweden 9C
New York, N. Y. ..9D, 10A, 10B, 11C, 12A, 14A, 14B, 17, 18A, 18B, 19C
Niagara, Fort 11C, 11D, 17, 18A, 19C
Nicaragua 32B
Norfolk, Va. 12A, 26A
Normandy Landings 47D
North Atlantic Treaty Organization (NATO)......50B
North Carolina 17
Northern Pacific Railroad 31B
Nova Scotia 7C, 7D, 9C, 10B 11C
Ohio River 6B, 14B, 20B
Okinawa, Battle of 49C
Old Spanish Trail 20A
Ontario, Lake 6B, 11C, 18B
Orange, Fort (Albany) 9C
Oregon Country 16B
Oregon Territory 22B, 23C
Oregon Trail 20A
Organization of American States (OAS) 50B
Oswego, N. Y. 17
Palo Alto, Battle of 21B
Pearl Harbor 48B
Pea Ridge, Battle of 24A
Pennsylvania 9D, 10B, 11C
Perryville, Battle of 24A
Petersburg, Battle of 27C
Philadelphia, Pa. 12A, 14A
Philippine Islands 5B, 32A, 48B, 49C, 52A, 52B
Plains of Abraham 11C
Pitt, Fort 15D
Plymouth 6B, 8B
Plymouth Colony 9C
Plymouth Company 8A
Plymouth Council for New England 8B
Pony Express 30A
Port Hudson, Battle of 24B
Port Republic, Battle of 26A
Potomac River 26A
Proclamation Line of 1763....16B
Puerto Rico 32A, 32B
Pulaski, Fort 24A
Quebec 6B, 10A, 11C, 11D
Queen Anne's War 10A
Queenston, Battle of 18A
Red River Basin 16B
Refugio, Battle of 21A
Resaca de la Palma, Battle of 21B
Rhode Island 9D
Richmond, Va. 12A, 24A, 25C, 26A, 27C
Rio Grande 6B, 21A, 21B
Roanoke Settlement 6B, 7A
Rocky Mountains 6B, 20A, 30A, 30B, 31C
Ross, Fort 13D
Sacramento, Calif. 20A
Saint Augustine, Fla. 6B, 7A, 9D, 10A, 10B, 11D
Saint Joseph, Mo. 30A
Salt Lake City, Utah 20A, 30A, 30B
Saint Lawrence River ...5A, 10A, 10B, 11C, 14B, 18B
Saint Louis, Mo. ...6B, 20A, 20B
Saint Mihiel Offensive 41C
Salem, Mass. 12A
San Antonio, Texas 7A, 11D, 21A, 21B
San Diego, Calif. 13D, 21B
San Francisco, Calif. 13D, 20A, 30A, 30B, 31C
San Gabriel (mission) 13D
San Jacinto, Battle of 21A
San Jose (mission) 13D
San Juan Bautista (mission) 13D
San Juan Capistrano (mission) 13D
San Juan Hill, Battle of 32A
San Luis Obispo (mission) ..1
San Luis Rey (mission) 1
San Pascual, Battle of 2
San Salvador 5A,
Santa Barbara (mission) 1
Santa Clara (mission) 1
Santa Cruz (mission) 1
Santa Fe, N. Mex. 6B, 11D, 20A, 2
Santa Fe Trail 2
Sarajevo, Yugo 4
Saratoga, N. Y. 10B, 1
Savannah, Ga. 10B, 12 14B, 1
Saylers Creek, Battle of 2
Seven Days Battles 2
Seven Years' War 1
Shenandoah Valley, Va. 26A, 26B, 2
Shiloh, Battle of 24
Smith, Fort 2
South Carolina 15C, 24A, 2
South Pass 2
Southeast Asia Treaty Organization (SEATO)....5
Southern Pacific Railroad 30B, 3
South Mountain, Battle of....2
Space Surveillance System (SPASUR) 5
Spanish Trail 11D, 13D, 2
Spotsylvania, Battle of 2
Stoney Creek, Battle of 1
Sumter, Fort 24
Sutter's, Fort ....
Texas 7C, 7D, 21A, 2
Texas Annexation 1
Thames, Battle of the 1
Three Chopped Way 2
Ticonderoga, Fort 11C, 14, 14
Tippecanoe, Battle of 18
Tombstone, Ariz. 3
Tordesillas, Treaty of 5
Trenton, Battle of 14
Tripoli blockade and bombardment 19
Tucson, Ariz. 11D, 20
Union Pacific Railroad 30
United Nations 50
Utah Territory 22
Valley Forge, Pa. 15
Vandalia, Ill. 20
Venango, Fort 11
Veracruz, Mexico 21B, 32
Vermont ....
Vicksburg, Battle of 24A, 24B, 2
Vietnam Conflict 53
Vincennes, Ind. 11D, 15
Virginia 12
Virginia City, Nev. 30
Virginia Claim ....
Virginia Company of London 8
Washington, D. C. 19C, 26, 26B, 27
Washington Territory 23
Watauga Settlements 12
Western Front 40
West Point 15
White Plains, Battle of 14
Wilderness, Battle of 27
Wilderness Rd. 20
Willamette Valley Settlement 20
William Henry, Fort 11
Williamsburg, Va. 12A, 26
Winchester, Battle of 26, 26B, 27
Yorktown, Va. 15C, 26